THE
POETICAL WORKS
OF
JOHN SCOTT ESQ.

Ang. Kauffman Inv.   F. Bartolozzi Sculp.

Published as the Act directs Octr 1st 1781 by James Buckland

THE
POETICAL WORKS
OF
JOHN SCOTT ESQ.

LONDON
Printed for J. Buckland,

MDCCLXXXII.

S.B.N. - GB: 576.02124.5

Republished in 1969 by Gregg International Publishers Limited
Westmead, Farnborough, Hants., England.

Printed in Offset by Kingprint Limited
Teddington, Middx., England.

ADVERTISEMENT.

SUCH of the following Pieces as were formerly publifhed having been honoured with general approbation, any apology for reprinting them muft be unneceffary. The others, which conftitute the principal part of this Volume, it is apprehended, are not of inferior merit; and the whole may perhaps afford an innocent and agreeable amufement to the Lovers of Nature and Poetry.

AMWELL, 1782.

A

C O N T E N T S.

CONTENTS.

6   An

LIST of the ENGRAVINGS.

E R R A T A.

Notwithstanding the Author's utmost attention to the Press, the following Mistakes unfortunately escaped his notice.

Page 17, Line 6, for *wane* read *wain*
——126, ⎫ for *Essay on Oriental Poetry*, read *Essay on*
——134, ⎭   the *Poetry of the Eastern Nations.*
——160, Line 5, for *Bid* read *Bade*
——237, Line 13, for *stern* read *severe*
——295, Line 4, for *turn'd* read *turn*

*** The following erroneous assertion was occasioned by a culpable dependance on Memory, viz.

Page 290, EURIPIDES is said to have been termed, by COLLINS, the *Priest of Pity*. That appellation may have been given to the Grecian Poet by some other Writer, but it is not by COLLINS.

MORAL

ECLOGUES.

At fecura quies, et nefcia fallere vita,
Dives opum variarum ; at latis otia fundis,
Speluncæ, vivique lacus ; at frigida Tempe,
Mugitufque boum, mollefque fub arbore fomni
Non abfunt. Illic faltus, ac luftra ferarum,
Et patiens operum parvoque affueta juventus,
Sacra deûm, fanctique patres : extrema per illos
Juftitia excedens terris veftigia fecit.

VIRG. Georg. II. l. 467.

ADVERTISEMENT.

The moſt rational definition of Paſtoral Poetry
ſeems to be that of the learned and ingenious Dr.
JOHNSON, in the 37th Number of his RAMBLER.
' Paſtoral,' ſays he, ' being the repreſentation of an
' Action or Paſſion, by its effects on a Country Life,
' has nothing peculiar, but its confinement to Rural
' Imagery, without which it ceaſes to be Paſtoral.'
This Theory the Author of the following Eclogues
has endeavoured to exemplify.

2

Stothard del.   Heath sculp.

E C L O G U E   I.

THERON; or, the Praife of RURAL LIFE.

SCENE, a Heath:

Seafon, SPRING; Time, MORNING.

F AIR Spring o'er Nature held her gentleft fway;
   Fair Morn diffus'd around her brighteft ray;
Thin mifts hung hovering on the diftant trees,
Or roll'd from off the fields before the breeze.
The Shepherd THERON watch'd his fleecy train,
Beneath a broad oak, on the graffy plain.
A heath's green wild lay pleafant to his view,
With fhrubs and field-flowers deck'd of varied hue:

There

There hawthorns tall their filver bloom difclos'd,

Here flexile broom's bright yellow interpos'd;

There purple orchis, here pale daifies fpread,

And fweet May-lilies richeft odour fhed.

From many a copfe and bloffom'd orchard near,

The voice of birds melodious charm'd the ear;

There fhrill the lark and foft the linnet fung,

And loud through air the throftle's mufick rung.

The gentle Swain the chearful fcene admir'd;

The chearful fcene the fong of joy infpir'd.

‘ Chant on,’ he cry'd, ‘ ye warblers on the fpray !

‘ Bleat on, ye flocks, that in the paftures play !

‘ Low on, ye herds, that range the dewy vales !

‘ Murmur, ye rills ! and whifper foft, ye gales !

‘ How bleft my lot, in thefe fweet fields affign'd,

‘ Where Peace and Leifure footh the tuneful mind;

‘ Where yet fome pleafing veftiges remain

‘ Of unperverted Nature's golden reign,

‘ When Love and Virtue rang'd Arcadian fhades,

‘ With undefigning youths and artlefs maids !

‘ For

' For us, though deftin'd to a later time,

' A lefs luxuriant foil, lefs genial clime,

' For us the country boafts enough to charm,

' In the wild woodland or the cultur'd farm.

' Come, CYNTHIO, come! in town no longer ftay;

' From crouds, and noife, and folly, hafte away!

' The fields, the meads, the trees, are all in bloom,

' The vernal fhow'rs awake a rich perfume.

' Where DAMON's manfion, by the glaffy ftream,

' Rears its white walls that thro' green willows gleam,

' Annual the neighbours hold their fhearing-day;

' And blithe youths come, and nymphs in neat array:

' Thofe fhear their fheep, upon the fmooth turf laid,

' In the broad plane's or trembling poplar's fhade;

' Thefe for their friends th'expected feaft provide,

' Beneath cool bowers along th' inclofure's fide.

' To view the toil, the glad repaft to fhare,

' Thy DELIA, my MELANIA, fhall be there;

' Each, kind and faithful to her faithful fwain,

' Loves the calm pleafures of the paftoral plain.

' Come,

‘ Come, CYNTHIO, come! If towns and crouds invite,

‘ And noife and folly promife high delight ;

‘ Soon the tir'd foul difgufted turns from thefe—

‘ The rural profpect, only, long can pleafe !’

E C L O G U E   II.

PALEMON; or, BENEVOLENCE.

SCENE, a Wood-fide on the Brow of a Hill:

Seafon, SUMMER; Time, FORENOON.

BRIGHT fleecy clouds flew fcattering o'er the fky,
    And fhorten'd fhadows fhew'd that noon was nigh;
When two young Shepherds, in the upland fhade,
Their liftlefs limbs upon the greenfward laid.
Surrounding groves the wandering fight confin'd—
All, fave where, weftward, one wide landfcape fhin'd.
Down in the dale were neat inclofures feen,
The winding hedge-row, and the thicket green;
Rich marfhland next a glofſy level fhow'd,
And thro' grey willows filver rivers flow'd:
Beyond, high hills with towers and villas crown'd,
And waving forefts, form'd the profpect's bound.

      Sweet

Sweet was the covert where the Swains reclin'd !

There spread the wild rose, there the woodbine
     twin'd;

There stood green fern ; there, o'er the grassy
     ground,

Sweet camomile and alehoof crept around ;

And centaury red and yellow cinquefoil grew,

And scarlet campion, and cyanus blue ;

And tufted thyme, and marjoram's purple bloom,

And ruddy strawberries yielding rich perfume.

Gay flies their wings on each fair flower display'd,

And labouring bees a lulling murmur made.

Along the brow a path delightful lay ;

Slow by the youths PALEMON chanc'd to stray,

A Bard, who often to the rural throng,

At vacant hours rehears'd the moral song !

The song the Shepherds crav'd ; the Sage reply'd :

‘ As late my steps forsook the fountain side,

‘ Adown the green lane by the beechen grove,

‘ Their flocks young PIRONEL and LARVON drove ;

                  ‘ With

' With us perchance they'll reft awhile'—The Swains

Approach'd the fhade; their fheep fpread o'er the

    plains :

Silent they view'd the venerable man,

Whofe voice melodious thus the lay began.

' What ALCON fung where Evefham's vales extend,

' I fing; ye Swains, your pleas'd attention lend !

' There long with him the rural life I led,

' His fields I cultur'd, and his flocks I fed.

' Where, by the hamlet road upon the green,

' Stood pleafant cots with trees difpers'd between,

' Befide his door, as waving o'er his head

' A lofty elm its ruftling foliage fpread,

' Frequent he fat; while all the village train

' Prefs'd round his feat, and liften'd to his ftrain.

' And once of fair Benevolence he fung,

' And thus the tuneful numbers left his tongue :

" Ye youth of Avon's banks, of Bredon's groves,

" Sweet fcenes, where Plenty reigns, and Pleafure

    " roves !

                " Woo

" Woo to your bowers Benevolence the fair,

" Kind as your foil, and gentle as your air.

" She comes ! her tranquil ftep, and placid eye,

" Fierce Rage, fell Hate, and ruthlefs Avarice fly.

" She comes! her heav'nly fmiles, with powerful

  " charm,

" Smooth Care's rough brow, and reft Toil's weary

  " arm.

" She comes ! ye Shepherds, importune her ftay !

" While your fair farms exuberant wealth difplay,

" While herds and flocks their annual increafe yield,

" And yellow harvefts load the fruitful field ;

" Beneath grim Want's inexorable reign,

" Pale Sicknefs, oft, and feeble Age complain !

" Why this unlike allotment, fave to fhow,

" That who poffefs, poffefs but to beftow ?"

 PALEMON ceas'd.—' Sweet is the found of gales

' Amid green ofiers in the winding vales ;

' Sweet is the lark's loud note on funny hills,

' What time fair Morn the fky with fragrance fills ;

      ' Sweet

' Sweet is the nightingale's love-foothing ftrain,

' Heard by ftill waters on the moonlight plain !

' But not the gales that thro' green ofiers play,

' Nor lark's nor nightingale's melodious lay,

' Pleafe like fmooth numbers by the Mufe in-

  ' fpir'd!'—

Larvon reply'd, and homeward all retir'd.

E C L O G U E III.

ARMYN; or, THE DISCONTENTED.

SCENE, a Valley:

Seafon, SUMMER; Time, AFTERNOON.

SUMMER o'er heav'n diffus'd fereneft blue,
 And painted earth with many a pleafing hue;
When ARMYN mus'd the vacant hour away,
Where willows o'er him wav'd their pendent fpray.
Cool was the fhade, and cool the paffing gale,
And fweet the profpect of the adjacent vale:
The fertile foil, profufe of plants, beftow'd
The crowfoot's gold, the trefoil's purple fhow'd,
And fpiky mint rich fragrance breathing round,
And meadfweet tall with tufts of flowrets crown'd,
And comfry white, and hoary filver-weed,
The bending ofier, and the ruftling reed.

There,

There, where clear ſtreams about green iſlands
    ſpread,

Fair flocks and herds, the wealth of ARMYN, fed ;

There, on the hill's ſoft ſlope, delightful view !

Fair fields of corn, the wealth of ARMYN, grew.

His ſturdy hinds, a ſlow laborious band,

Swept their bright ſcythes along the level land :

Blithe youths and maidens nimbly near them paſt,

And the thick ſwarth in careleſs wind-rows caſt.

Full on the landſcape ſhone the weſtering ſun,

When thus the Swain's ſoliloquy begun :

   ‘ Haſte down, O Sun ! and cloſe the tedious day :

‘ Time, to the unhappy, ſlowly moves away.

‘ Not ſo, to me, in Roden's ſylvan bowers,

‘ Paſs'd Youth's ſhort bliſsful reign of careleſs hours;

‘ When to my view the fancy'd future lay,

‘ A region ever tranquil, ever gay.

‘ O then, what ardors did my breaſt inflame !

‘ What thoughts were mine, of friendſhip, love, and
    ‘ fame !

                         ‘ How

' How taftelefs life, now all its joys are try'd,

' And warm purfuits in dull repofe fubfide !'

He paus'd : his clofing words ALBINO heard,

As down the ftream his little boat he fteer'd;

His hand releas'd the fail, and dropt the oar,

And moor'd the light fkiff on the fedgy fhore.

' Ceafe, gentle Swain,' he faid ; ' no more, in

    ' vain,

' Thus make paft pleafure caufe of prefent pain !

' Ceafe, gentle Swain,' he faid ; ' from thee, alone,

' Are youth's bleft hours and fancy'd profpects flown ?

' Ah, no !—remembrance to my view reftores

' Dear native fields, which now my foul deplores ;

' Rich hills and vales, and pleafant village fcenes

' Of oaks whofe wide arms ftretch'd o'er daified greens,

' And wind-mill's fails flow-circling in the breeze,

' And cottage-walls envelop'd half with trees—

' Sweet fcenes, where Beauty met the ravifh'd

    ' fight,

' And Mufic often gave the ear delight ;

             ' Where

' Where DELIA's fmile, and MIRA's tuneful fong,

' And DAMON's converfe, charm'd the youthful

  ' throng !

' How chang'd, alas, how chang'd !—O'er all our

  ' plains,

' Proud NORVAL, now, in lonely grandeur reigns;

' His wide-fpread park a wafte of verdure lies,

' And his vaft villa's glittering roofs arife.

' For me, hard fate !—But fay, fhall I complain ?

' Thefe limbs yet active Life's fupport obtain.

' Let us, or good or evil as we fhare,

' That thankful prize, and this with patience bear.'

The foft reproach touch'd ARMYN's gentle breaft ;

His alter'd brow a placid fmile expreft.

' Calm as clear ev'nings after vernal rains,

' When all the air a rich perfume retains,

' My mind,' faid he, ' its murmurs driv'n away,

' Feels Truth's full force, and bows to Reafon's fway !'

He ceas'd : the fun, with horizontal beams,

Gilt the green mountains, and the glittering ftreams.

     Slow

Slow down the tide before the finking breeze,

Albino's white fail gleam'd among the trees;

Slow down the tide his winding courfe he bore

To watry Talgar's afpin-fhaded fhore.

Slow crofs the valley, to the fouthern hill,

The fteps of Armyn fought the diftant vill,

Where thro' tall elms the mofs-grown turret rofe;

And his fair manfion offer'd fweet repofe.

E C L O G U E   IV.

LYCORON; or, THE UNHAPPY.

SCENE, a Valley:

Seafon, AUTUMN; Time, EVENING.

THE matron, Autumn, held her fober reign
   O'er fading foliage on the ruffet plain :
Mild Evening came; the moon began to rife,
And fpread pale luftre o'er unclouded fkies.
'Twas filence all—fave, where along the road
The flow wane grating bore its cumb'rous load;
Save, where broad rivers roll'd their waves away,
And fcreaming herons fought their watry prey—
When haplefs DAMON, in Algorno's vale,
Pour'd his foft forrows on the paffing gale.

  ' That grace of fhape, that elegance of air,
 ' That blooming face fo exquifitely fair;

C

                                ' That

' That eye of brightnefs bright as morning's ray,

' That fmile of foftnefs foft as clofing day,

' Which bound my foul to thee; all, all are fled—

' All loft in dreary manfions of the dead !

' Ev'n him, whom diftance from his Love divides,

' Toil'd on fcorch'd fands, or toft on rolling tides,

' Kind Hope ftill chears, ftill paints, to footh his pain,

' The happy moment when they meet again.

' Far worfe my lot ! of Hope bereft, I mourn !—

' The parted fpirit never can return !'

Thus Damon fpoke, as in the cyprefs gloom

He hung lamenting o'er his Delia's tomb.

In the ftill valley where they wander'd near,

Two gentle Shepherds chanc'd his voice to hear:

Lycoron's head Time's hand had filver'd o'er,

And Milo's cheek Youth's rofy blufhes bore.

' How mournful,' faid Lycoron, ' flows that ftrain !

' It brings paft miferies to my mind again.

' When the blithe Village, on the vernal green,

' Sees its fair Daughters in the dance convene ;

And

' And Youth's light ftep in fearch of Pleafure ftrays,

' And his fond eyes on Beauty fix their gaze ;

' Shouldft thou then, lingering midft the lovely

    ' train,

' Wifh fome young Charmer's eafy heart to gain,

' Mark well, that Reafon Love's purfuit approve,

' Ere thy foft arts her tender paffions move :

' Elfe, tho' thy thoughts in Summer regions range,

' Calm funny climes that feem to fear no change ;

' Rude Winter's rage will foon the fcene deform,

' Dark with thick cloud, and rough with battering

    ' ftorm !'

' When parents interdict, and friends diffuade,

' The prudent cenfure, and the proud upbraid ;

' Think ! all their efforts then fhalt thou difdain,

' Thy faith, thy conftancy, unmov'd, maintain?

' To Ifca's fields, me once Ill-fortune led ;

' In Ifca's fields, her flocks ZELINDA fed :

' There oft, when Ev'ning, on the filent plain,

' Commenc'd with fweet ferenity her reign,

    ' Along

‘ Along green groves, or down the winding dales,

‘ The Fair-one liften’d to my tender tales ;

‘ Then when her mind, or doubt, or fear, diftreft,

‘ And doubt, or fear, her anxious eyes expreft,

“ O no !” faid I, “ let oxen quit the mead,

“ With climbing goats on craggy cliffs to feed ;

“ Before the hare the hound affrighted fly,

“ And larks purfue the falcon through the fky ;

“ Streams ceafe to flow, and winds to ftir the lake,

“ If I, unfaithful, ever thee forfake !—”

‘ What my tongue utter’d then, my heart believ’d :

‘ O wretched heart, felf-flatter’d and deceiv’d !

‘ Fell Slander’s arts the Virgin’s fame accus’d ;

‘ And whom my love had chofe, my pride refus’d.

‘ For me, that cheek did tears of grief diftain ?

‘ To me, that voice in anguifh plead in vain ?

‘ What fiend relentlefs then my foul poffeft ?

‘ Oblivion hide ! for ever hide the reft !

‘ Too well her innocence and truth were prov’d ;

‘ Too late my pity and my juftice mov’d !

He

He ceas'd, with groans that more than words
 expreſt;

And ſmote in agony his aged breaſt.

His friend reply'd not; but, with ſoothing ſtrains

Of ſolemn muſic, ſought to eaſe his pains:

Soft flow'd the notes, as gales that waft perfume

From cowſlip meads, or linden boughs in bloom.

Peace o'er their minds a calm compoſure caſt;

And ſlowly down the ſhadowy vale in penſive mood
 they paſt.

ECLOGUE IV

ELEGIES

DESCRIPTIVE and MORAL.

Stothard del.   Blake sc.

There is, who deems all climes, all seasons fair,
Contentment, thankful for the gift of life!   Elegy IV.

ELEGY I.

Written at the APPROACH of SPRING.

STERN Winter hence with all his train removes,
　And cheerful ſkies and limpid ſtreams are ſeen;
Thick-ſprouting foliage decorates the groves;
　Reviving herbage clothes the fields with green.

Yet lovelier ſcenes th' approaching months prepare;
　Kind Spring's full bounty ſoon will be diſplay'd;
The ſmile of beauty ev'ry vale ſhall wear;
　The voice of ſong enliven ev'ry ſhade.

O Fancy,

O Fancy, paint not coming days too fair !
   Oft for the profpects fprightly May fhould yield,
Rain-pouring clouds have darken'd all the air,
   Or fnows untimely whiten'd o'er the field :

But fhould kind Spring her wonted bounty fhow'r,
   The fmile of beauty, and the voice of fong;
If gloomy thought the human mind o'erpow'r,
   Ev'n vernal hours glide unenjoy'd along.

I fhun the fcenes where madd'ning paffion raves,
   Where Pride and Folly high dominion hold,
And unrelenting Avarice drives her flaves
   O'er proftrate Virtue in purfuit of gold.

The graffy lane, the wood-furrounded field,
   The rude ftone fence with fragrant wall-flow'rs gay,
The clay-built cot, to me more pleafure yield
   Than all the pomp imperial domes difplay :

                         And

And yet even here, amid thefe fecret fhades,

  Thefe fimple fcenes of unreprov'd delight,

Affliétion's iron hand my breaft invades,

  And Death's dread dart is ever in my fight.

While genial funs to genial fhow'rs fucceed,

  (The air all mildnefs, and the earth all bloom);

While herds and flocks range fportive o'er the mead,

  Crop the fweet herb, and fnuff the rich perfume;

O why alone to haplefs man deny'd

  To tafte the blifs inferior beings boaft?

O why this fate, that fear and pain divide

  His few fhort hours on earth's delightful coaft?

Ah ceafe—no more of Providence complain!

  'Tis fenfe of guilt that wakes the mind to woe,

Gives force to fear, adds energy to pain,

  And palls each joy by Heav'n indulg'd below:

                                Why

Why elfe the fmiling infant-train fo bleft,

    Ere ill propenfion ripens into fin,

Ere wild defire inflames the youthful breaft,

    And dear-bought knowledge ends the peace within ?

As to the bleating tenants of the field,

    As to the fportive warblers on the trees,

To them their joys fincere the feafons yield,

    And all their days and all their profpects pleafe ;

Such mine, when firft, from London's crowded ftreets,

    Rov'd my young fteps to Surry's wood-crown'd hills,

O'er new-blown meads that breath'd a thoufand fweets,

    By fhady coverts and by chryftal rills.

O happy hours, beyond recov'ry fled !

    What fhare I now that can your lofs repay,

While o'er my mind thefe glooms of thought are fpread,

    And veil the light of life's meridian ray ?

                               Is

Is there no Power this darkneſs to remove?

 The long-loſt joys of Eden to reſtore?

Or raiſe our views to happier ſeats above,

 Where fear and pain and death ſhall be no more?

Yes, thoſe there are who know a SAVIOUR's love

 The long-loſt joys of Eden can reſtore,

And raiſe their views to happier ſeats above,

 Where fear and pain and death ſhall be no more:

Theſe grateful ſhare the gifts of Nature's hand;

 And in the varied ſcenes that round them ſhine

(Minute and beautiful, or rude and grand),

 Admire th' amazing workmanſhip divine.

Blows not a flow'ret in th' enamel'd vale,

 Shines not a pebble where the riv'let ſtrays,

Sports not an inſect on the ſpicy gale,

 But claims their wonder and excites their praiſe.

For

For them ev'n vernal Nature looks more gay,

　　For them more lively hues the fields adorn;

To them more fair the faireſt ſmile of Day,

　　To them more ſweet the ſweeteſt breath of Morn.

They feel the blifs that Hope and Faith ſupply;

　　They paſs ſerene th' appointed hours that bring

The Day that wafts them to the realms on high,

　　The Day that centers in Eternal Spring.

E L E G Y   II.

Written in the HOT WEATHER, *July*, 1757.

THree hours from noon the paffing fhadow fhows,
 The fultry breeze glides faintly o'er the plains,
The dazzling Ether fierce and fiercer glows,
 And human nature fcarce its rage fuftains.

Now ftill and vacant is the dufty ftreet,
 And ftill and vacant all yon fields extend,
Save where thofe fwains, opprefs'd with toil and heat,
 The graffy harveft of the mead attend.

Loft is the lively afpect of the ground,
 Low are the fprings, the reedy ditches dry;
No verdant fpot in all the vale is found,
 Save what yon ftream's unfailing ftores fupply.

         Where

Where are the flow'rs, the garden's rich array?

   Where is their beauty, where their fragrance fled?

Their ftems relax, faft fall their leaves away,

   They fade and mingle with their dufty bed:

All but the natives of the torrid zone,

   What Afric's wilds, or Peru's fields difplay,

Pleas'd with a clime that imitates their own,.

   They lovelier bloom beneath the parching ray.

Where is wild Nature's heart-reviving fong,

   That fill'd in genial fpring the verdant bow'rs?

Silent in gloomy woods the feather'd throng

   Pine thro' this long, long courfe of fultry hours.

Where is the dream of blifs by Summer brought?

   The walk along the riv'let-water'd vale?

The field with verdure clad, with fragrance fraught?

   The fun mild-beaming, and the fanning gale?

The

The weary foul Imagination chears,

    Her pleafing colours paint the future gay:

Time paffes on, the truth itfelf appears,

    The pleafing colours inftant fade away.

In diff'rent feafons diff'rent joys we place,

    And thefe will Spring fupply, and Summer thefe;

Yet frequent ftorms the bloom of Spring deface,

    And Summer fcarcely brings a day to pleafe.

O for fome fecret fhady cool recefs,

    Some Gothic dome o'erhung with darkfome trees,

Where thick damp walls this raging heat reprefs,

    Where the long aifle invites the lazy breeze!

But why thefe plaints?—reflect, nor murmur more—

    Far worfe their fate in many a foreign land,

The Indian tribes on Darien's fwampy fhore,

    The Arabs wand'ring over Mecca's fand.

                             Far

Far worſe, alas! the feeling mind ſuſtains,

     Rack'd with the poignant pangs of fear or ſhame;

The hopeleſs lover bound in Beauty's chains,

     The bard whom Envy robs of hard-earn'd fame;

He, who a father or a mother mourns,

     Or lovely conſort loſt in early bloom;

He, whom fell FEBRIS, rapid Fury! burns,

     Or PHTHISIS ſlow leads ling'ring to the tomb—

Leſt Man ſhould ſink beneath the preſent pain;

     Leſt Man ſhould triumph in the preſent joy;

For him th' unvarying laws of Heav'n ordain,

     Hope in his ills, and to his bliſs alloy.

Fierce and oppreſſive is the heat we bear,

     Yet not unuſeful to our humid ſoil;

Thence ſhall our fruits a richer flavour ſhare,

     Thence ſhall our plains with riper harveſts ſmile.

                        Reflect,

Reflect, nor murmur more—for, good in all,

    Heaven gives the due degrees of drought or rain;

Perhaps ere morn refreshing show'rs may fall,

    Nor soon yon sun rise blazing fierce again :

Ev'n now behold the grateful change at hand!

    Hark, in the East loud blust'ring gales arise;

Wide and more wide the dark'ning clouds expand,

    And distant lightnings flash along the skies !

O, in the awful concert of the storm,

    While hail and rain and wind and thunder join;

May deep-felt gratitude my soul inform,

    May joyful songs of rev'rent praise be mine !

D

E L E G Y III.

Written in HARVEST.

FAREWELL the pleafant violet-fcented fhade,
  The primros'd hill, and daify-mantled mead;
The furrow'd land, with fpringing corn array'd;
  The funny wall, with bloomy branches fpread:

Farewell the bow'r with blufhing rofes gay;
  Farewell the fragrant trefoil-purpled field;
Farewell the walk through rows of new-mown hay,
  When ev'ning breezes mingled odours yield:

Of thefe no more—now round the lonely farms,
  Where jocund Plenty deigns to fix her feat;
Th' autumnal landfcape op'ning all its charms,
  Declares kind Nature's annual work complete.

In

In diff'rent parts what diff'rent views delight,
  Where on neat ridges waves the golden grain;
Or where the bearded barley dazzling white,
  Spreads o'er the steepy slope or wide champaign.

The smile of Morning gleams along the hills,
  And wakeful Labour calls her sons abroad;
They leave with chearful look their lowly vills,
  And bid the fields resign their ripen'd load.

In various tasks engage the rustic bands,
  And here the scythe, and there the sickle wield;
Or rear the new-bound sheaves along the lands,
  Or range in heaps the swarths upon the field.

Some build the shocks, some load the spacious wains,
  Some lead to shelt'ring barns the fragrant corn;
Some form tall ricks, that tow'ring o'er the plains
  For many a mile, the homestead yards adorn.—

The rattling car with verdant branches crown'd,

   The joyful fwains that raife the clam'rous fong,

Th' inclofure gates thrown open all around,

   The ftubble peopled by the gleaning throng,

Soon mark glad harveft o'er—Ye rural Lords,

   Whofe wide domains o'er Albion's ifle extend;

Think whofe kind hand your annual wealth affords,

   And bid to Heaven your grateful praife afcend!

For tho' no gift fpontaneous of the ground

   Rofe thefe fair crops that made your vallies fmile,

Tho' the blithe youth of every hamlet round

   Purfued for thefe thro' many a day their toil;

Yet what avail your labours or your cares?

   Can all your labours, all your cares, fupply

Bright funs, or foft'ning fhow'rs, or tepid airs,

   Or one indulgent influence of the fky?

                        For

For Providence decrees, that we obtain

 With toil each bleffing deftin'd to our ufe;

But means to teach us, that our toil is vain

 If He the bounty of his hand refufe.

Yet, Albion, blame not what thy crime demands,

 While this fad truth the blufhing Mufe betrays—

More frequent echoes o'er thy harveft lands,

 The voice of Riot than the voice of Praife.

Prolific tho' thy fields, and mild thy clime,

 Realms fam'd for fields as rich, for climes as fair,

Have fall'n the prey of Famine, War, and Time,

 And now no femblance of their glory bear.

Afk Paleftine, proud Afia's early boaft,

 Where now the groves that pour'd her wine and oil;

Where the fair towns that crown'd her wealthy coaft;

 Where the glad fwains that till'd her fertile foil:

     Afk,

Aſk, and behold, and mourn her hapleſs fall!

 Where roſe fair towns, where toil'd the jocund ſwain,

Thron'd on the naked rock and mould'ring wall,

 Pale Want and Ruin hold their dreary reign.

Where Jordan's vallies ſmil'd in living green,

 Where Sharon's flow'rs diſcloſ'd their varied hues,

The wand'ring pilgrim views the alter'd ſcene,

 And drops the tear of pity as he views.

Aſk Grecia, mourning o'er her ruin'd tow'rs;

 Where now the proſpects charm'd her bards of old,

Her corn-clad mountains and Elyſian bow'rs,

 And ſilver ſtreams thro' fragrant meadows roll'd.

Where Freedom's praiſe along the vale was heard,

 And town to town return'd the fav'rite found;

Where Patriot War her awful ſtandard rear'd,

 And brav'd the millions Perſia pour'd around:

        There

There Freedom's praife no more the valley chears,

 There Patriot War no more her banner waves;

Nor bard, nor fage, nor martial chief appears,

 But ftern barbarians rule a land of flaves.

Of mighty realms are fuch the poor remains?

 Of mighty realms that fell, when mad with pow'r,

They call'd for Vice to revel on their plains;

 The monfter doom'd their offspring to devour!

O Albion! wouldft thou fhun their mournful fate,

 To fhun their follies and their crimes be thine;

And woo to linger in thy fair retreat,

 The radiant Virtues, progeny divine!

Fair Truth, with dauntlefs eye and afpect bland;

 Sweet Peace, whofe brow no angry frown deforms;

Soft Charity, with ever-open hand;

 And Courage, calm amid furrounding ftorms.

D 4

O lovely

O lovely Train ! O hafte to grace our Ifle !

   So may the Pow'r who ev'ry bleffing yields,

Bid on her clime fereneft feafons fmile,

   And crown with annual wealth her far-fam'd fields.

E L E G Y IV.

Written at the Approach of WINTER.

THE Sun far fouthward bends his annual way,
 The bleak North-eaft Wind lays the forefts bare,
The fruit ungather'd quits the naked fpray,
 And dreary Winter reigns o'er earth and air.

No mark of vegetable life is feen,
 No bird to bird repeats his tuneful call;
Save the dark leaves of fome rude evergreen,
 Save the lone red-breaft on the mofs-grown wall.

Where are the fprightly profpects Spring fupply'd,
 The may-flower'd hedges fcenting every breeze;
The white flocks fcatt'ring o'er the mountain's fide,
 The woodlarks warbling on the blooming trees?

Where

Where is gay Summer's fportive infect train,

    That in green fields on painted pinions play'd?

The herd at morn wide-pafturing o'er the plain,

    Or throng'd at noon-tide in the willow fhade?

Where is brown Autumn's ev'ning mild and ftill,

    What time the ripen'd corn frefh fragrance yields,

What time the village peoples all the hill,

    And loud fhouts echo o'er the harveft fields?

To former fcenes our fancy thus returns,

    To former fcenes that little pleas'd when here!

Our Winter chills us, and our Summer burns,

    Yet we diflike the changes of the year.

To happier lands then reftlefs Fancy flies,

    Where Indian ftreams thro' green Savannahs flow;

Where brighter funs and ever tranquil fkies

    Bid new fruits ripen, and new flow'rets blow.

Let

Let Truth thefe fairer happier lands furvey—

 There frowning Months defcend in wat'ry ftorms;

Or Nature faints amid the blaze of day,

 And one brown hue the fun-burnt plain deforms,

There oft, as toiling in the fultry fields,

 Or homeward paffing on the fhadelefs way,

His joylefs life the weary lab'rer yields,

 And inftant drops beneath the deathful ray.

Who dreams of Nature, free from Nature's ftrife?

 Who dreams of conftant happinefs below?

The hope-flufh'd ent'rer on the ftage of life;

 The youth to knowledge unchaftis'd by woe.

For me, long toil'd on many a weary road,

 Led by falfe Hope in fearch of many a joy;

I find in Earth's bleak clime no bleft abode,

 No place, no feafon, facred from annoy:

For me, while Winter rages round the plains,

   With his dark days I human life compare ;

Not those more fraught with clouds and winds and rains

   Than this with pining pain and anxious care,

O ! whence this wond'rous turn of mind our fate—

   Whate'er the season or the place possest,

We ever murmur at our present state ;

   And yet the thought of parting breaks our rest?

Why else, when heard in Ev'ning's solemn gloom,

   Does the sad knell, that sounding o'er the plain

Tolls some poor lifeless body to the tomb,

   Thus thrill my breast with melancholy pain ?

The voice of Reason thunders in my ear :

   ' Thus thou, ere long, must join thy kindred clay ;

' No more those nostrils breathe the vital air,

   ' No more those eyelids open on the day !'—

                   O Winter,

O Winter, o'er me hold thy dreary reign !

 Spread wide thy ſkies in darkeſt horrors dreſt !

Of their dread rage no longer I'll complain,

 Nor aſk an Eden for a tranſient gueſt.

Enough has Heaven indulg'd of joy below,

 To tempt our tarriance in this lov'd retreat ;

Enough has Heaven ordain'd of uſeful woe,

 To make us languiſh for a happier ſeat.

There is, who deems all climes, all ſeaſons fair ;

 There is, who knows no reſtleſs paſſion's ſtrife ;

Contentment, ſmiling at each idle care ;

 Contentment, thankful for the gift of life !

She finds in Winter many a view to pleaſe ;

 The morning landſcape fring'd with froſt-work gay,

The ſun at noon ſeen thro' the leafleſs trees,

 The clear calm ether at the cloſe of day :

She

She marks th' advantage ſtorms and clouds beſtow,

 When bluſt'ring Caurus purifies the air ;

When moiſt Aquarius pours the fleecy ſnow,

 That makes th' impregnate glebe a richer harveſt

   bear :

She bids, for all, our grateful praiſe ariſe,

 To Him whoſe mandate ſpake the world to form ;

Gave Spring's gay bloom, and Summer's chearful ſkies,

 And Autumn's corn-clad field, and Winter's

   ſounding ſtorm.

E L E G Y;

WRITTEN AT

AMWELL in HERTFORDSHIRE,

MDCCLXVIII.

E L E G Y.

Written at AMWELL, 1768.

O Friend! though filent thus thy tongue remains,
   I read enquiry in thy anxious eye,
Why my pale cheek the frequent tear diftains,
   Why from my bofom burfts the frequent figh.

Long from thefe fcenes detain'd in diftant fields,
   My mournful tale perchance efcap'd thy ear:
Frefh grief to me the repetition yields;
   Thy kind attention gives thee right to hear!

Foe to the world's purfuit of wealth and fame,
   Thy THERON early from the world retir'd,
Left to the bufy throng each boafted aim,
   Nor aught, fave peace in folitude, defir'd.

E   A few

A few choice volumes there could oft engage,

　　A few choice friends there oft amus'd the day;

There his lov'd Parents' flow-declining age,

　　Life's calm unvary'd ev'ning, wore away.

Foe to the futile manners of the proud,

　　He chose an humble Virgin for his own;

A form with Nature's faireft gifts endow'd,

　　And pure as vernal bloffoms newly blown:

Her hand fhe gave, and with it gave a heart

　　By love engag'd, with gratitude impreft,

Free without folly, prudent without art,

　　With wit accomplifh'd, and with virtue bleft.

Swift pafs'd the hours; alas, to pafs no more!

　　Flown like the light clouds of a fummer's day!

One beauteous pledge the beauteous confort bore;

　　The fatal gift forbad the giver's ftay.

Ere

Ere twice the Sun perform'd his annual round,

In one fad fpot where kindred afhes lie,

O'er wife, and child, and parents, clos'd the ground;

The final home of Man ordain'd to die !

O ceafe at length, obtrufive Mem'ry ! ceafe,

Nor in my view the wretched hours retain,

That faw Difeafe on her dear life increafe,

And Med'cine's lenient arts effay'd in vain.

O the dread fcene ! (in mifery how fublime !)

Of Love's vain pray'rs to ftay her fleeting breath !

Sufpenfe that reftlefs watch'd the flight of Time,

And helplefs dumb Defpair awaiting Death !

O the dread fcene !--'Tis agony to tell,

How o'er the couch of pain declin'd my head;

And took from dying lips the long farewel,

The laft, laft parting, ere her fpirit fled.

' Reftore

' Reſtore her, Heaven, as from the grave retrieve—

   ' In each calm moment all things elſe reſign'd,

' Her looks, her language, ſhow how hard to leave

   ' The lov'd companion ſhe muſt leave behind.

' Reſtore her, Heaven! for once in mercy ſpare—'

   Thus Love's vain prayer in anguiſh interpos'd :

And ſoon Suſpenſe gave place to dumb Deſpair,

   And o'er the paſt, Death's ſable curtain clos'd—

In ſilence clos'd—My thoughts rov'd frantic round,

   No hope, no wiſh, beneath the ſun remain'd ;

Earth, air, and ſkies one diſmal waſte I found,

   One pale, dead, dreary blank, with horror ſtain'd.

O lovely flow'r, too fair for this rude clime !

   O lovely morn, too prodigal of light !

O tranſient beauties, blaſted in their prime !

   O tranſient glories, ſunk in ſudden night !

Sweet

Sweet Excellence, by all who knew thee mourn'd!
　　Where is that form, that mind, my foul admir'd;
That form, with every pleafing charm adorn'd;
　　That mind, with every gentle thought infpir'd?

The face with rapture view'd, I view no more;
　　The voice with rapture heard, no more I hear:
Yet the lov'd features Mem'ry's eyes explore;
　　Yet the lov'd accents fall on Mem'ry's ear.

Ah fad, fad change! (fad fource of daily pain)
　　That fenfe of lofs ineffable renews;
While my rack'd bofom heaves the figh in vain,
　　While my pale cheek the tear in vain bedews.

Still o'er the grave that holds the dear remains,
　　The mould'ring veil her fpirit left below,
Fond Fancy dwells, and pours funereal ftrains,
　　The foul-diffolving melody of woe.

　　　　　　Nor

Nor mine alone to bear this painful doom,

    Nor fhe alone the tear of Song obtains;

The Mufe of Blagdon*, o'er Constantia's tomb,

    In all the eloquence of grief complains.

My friend's fair hope, like mine, fo lately gain'd;

    His heart, like mine, in its true partner bleft;

Both from one caufe the fame diftrefs fuftain'd,

    The fame fad hours beheld us both diftreft.

O Human Life! how mutable, how vain!

    How thy wide forrows circumfcribe thy joy—

A funny ifland in a ftormy main,

    A fpot of azure in a cloudy fky!

All-gracious Heaven! fince Man, infatuate Man,

    Refts in thy works, too negligent of thee,

Lays for himfelf on earth his little plan,

    Dreads not, or diftant views mortality;

---

* See Verfes written at Sandgate Caftle, in memory of a Lady, by the late ingenious Dr. Langhorne.

                  'Tis

'Tis but to wake to nobler thought the foul,

   To roufe us ling'ring on earth's flowery plain,

To Virtue's path our wand'rings to controul,

   Affliction frowning comes, thy minifter of pain!

A M W E L L :

A

DESCRIPTIVE POEM.

5

J. Feary del.   W. Walls sculp

NW View of Amwell from London Road.

A M W E L L:

A

DESCRIPTIVE POEM.

THERE dwells a fond defire in human minds,
　　When pleas'd, their pleafure to extend to thofe
Of kindred tafte ; and thence th' inchanting arts
Of Picture and of Song, the femblance fair
Of Nature's forms produce. This fond defire

Prompts

Prompts me to fing the lonely fylvan fcenes

Of Amwell; which, fo oft in early youth,

While novelty enhanc'd their native charms,

Gave rapture to my foul; and often, ftill,

On life's calm moments fhed ferener joy.

Defcriptive Mufe! whofe hand along the ftream

Of ancient Thames, thro' Richmond's fhady groves,

And Sheen's fair vallies, once thy Thomson led*;

And once o'er green Carmarthen's woody dales,

And funny landfcapes of Campania's plain,

Thy other favour'd bard †; thou, who fo late,

In bowers by Clent's wild peaks ‡, to Shenstone's ear

Didft bring fweet ftrains of rural melody,

(Alas no longer heard!)—vouchfafe thine aid;

* Thomson, Author of the Seafons, refided part of his life near Richmond.

† Dyer, Author of Grongar Hill; The Ruins of Rome; and that excellent neglected poem, The Fleece.

‡ The Clent-hills adjoin to Hagley-park, and are not far diftant from the Leafowes.

From

From all our rich varieties of view,

What beſt may pleaſe, aſſiſt me to ſeleƈt,

With art diſpoſe, with energy deſcribe,

And its full image on the mind impreſs.

And ye, who e'er in theſe delightful fields

Conſum'd with me the ſocial hour, while I

Your walk conduƈted o'er their lovelieſt ſpots,

And on their faireſt objeƈts fix'd your ſight;

Accept this verſe, which may to memory call

That ſocial hour, and ſweetly varied walk !

And Thou, by ſtrong connubial union mine;

Mine, by the ſtronger union of the heart;

In whom the loſs of parents and of friends,

And Her, the firſt fair partner of my joys,

All recompens'd I find; whoſe preſence chears

The ſoft domeſtic ſcene; MARIA, come!

The Country calls us forth; blithe Summer's hand

Sheds fweeteft flowers, and Morning's brighteft fmile

Illumines earth and air ; MARIA, come !

By winding pathways thro' the waving corn,

We reach the airy point that profpect yields,

Not vaft and awful, but confin'd and fair ;

Not the black mountain and the foamy main ;

Not the throng'd city and the bufy port ;

But pleafant interchange of foft afcent,

And level plain, and growth of fhady woods,

And twining courfe of rivers clear, and fight

Of rural towns and rural cots, whofe roofs

Rife fcattering round, and animate the whole.

Far tow'rds the weft, clofe under fheltering hills,

In verdant meads, by Lee's cerulean ftream,

Hertford's grey towers* afcend ; the rude remains

---

* In the beginning of the Heptarchy, the town of Hertford
was accounted one of the principal cities of the Eaft Saxons,
where the kings of that province often kept their courts, and a
parliamentary council, or national fynod, was held, Sept. 24th,
673. *Chauncy's Hertfordfhire*, p. 237.

Of high antiquity, from wafte efcap'd

Of envious Time, and violence of War.

For War there once, fo tells th' hiftoric page,

Led Defolation's fteps : the hardy Dane,

By Avarice lur'd, o'er Ocean's ftormy wave,

To ravage Albion's plains, his favourite feat,

There fix'd awhile; and there his caftles rear'd

Among the trees; and there, beneath yon ridge

Of piny rocks, his conquering navy moor'd,

With idle fails furl'd on the yard, and oars

Recumbent on the flood, and ftreamers gay

Triumphant fluttering on the paffing winds.

In fear, the fhepherd on the lonely heath

Tended his fcanty flock; the ploughman turn'd,

In fear, his hafty furrow : oft the din

Of hoftile arms alarm'd the ear, and flames

Of plunder'd towns thro' night's thick gloom from far

Gleam'd difmal on the fight: till ALFRED came,

Till ALFRED, father of his people, came,

Lee's rapid tide into new channels turn'd,

And left a-ground the Danian fleet, and forc'd

The foe to speedy flight*.   Then Freedom's voice

Reviv'd the drooping swain; then Plenty's hand

Recloth'd the desart fields, and Peace and Love

Sat smiling by; as now they smiling sit,

Obvious to Fancy's eye, upon the side

Of yon bright sunny theatre of hills,

Where Bengeo's villas rise, and Ware-park's lawns

Spread their green surface, interspers'd with groves

Of broad umbrageous oak, and spiry pine,

Tall elm, and linden pale, and blossom'd thorn,

---

* Towards the latter end of the year 879, the Danes advanced to the borders of Mercia, and erected two forts at Hertford on the Lee, for the security of their ships, which they had brought up that river.   Here they were attacked by the Londoners, who were repulsed.   But Alfred advancing with his army, and viewing the nature of their situation, turned the course of the stream, so that their vessels were left on dry ground; a circumstance which terrified them to such a degree, that they abandoned their forts, and, flying towards the Severn, were pursued by Alfred as far as Quatbridge. *Smollet's Hist. of England*, 8vo *Edition*, vol. i. p. 182.

Breathing

Breathing mild fragrance, like the fpicy gales

Of Indian iflands.   On the ample brow,

Where that white temple rears its pillar'd front

Half hid with gloffy foliage, many a chief

Renown'd for martial deeds, and many a bard

Renown'd for fong, have pafs'd the rural hour.

The gentle FANSHAW* there, from " noife of camps,

" From courts difeafe retir'd †," delighted view'd

The gaudy garden fam'd in WOTTON's page ‡;

* Sir RICHARD FANSHAW, tranflator of Guarini's Paftor Fido, the Lufiad of Camoens, &c.   He was fon of Sir Henry Fanfhaw of Ware-Park, and is faid to have refided much there. He was ambaffador to Portugal, and afterwards to Spain, and died at Madrid in 1666.   His body was brought to England and interred in Ware church, where his monument is ftill exifting. In Cibber's Lives of the Poets, it is erroneoufly afferted that he was buried in All-Saints church, Hertford.

† The words marked with inverted commas are part of a ftanza of Fanfhaw's.

‡ See Reliquiæ Wottonianæ, where the author makes a particular mention of the garden of Sir Henry Fanfhaw at Ware-park, " as a delicate and diligent curiofity," remarkable for the nice arrangement of its flowers.

F   Or

Or in the verdant maze, or cool arcade,

Sat mufing, and from fmooth Italian ftrains

The foft GUARINI's amorous lore transfus'd

Into rude Britith verfe. The warrior's arm

Now refts from toil; the poet's tuneful tongue

In filence lies; frail Man his lov'd domains

Soon quits for ever! they themfelves, by courfe

Of Nature often, or caprice of Art,

Experience change: even here, 'tis faid of old

Steep rocky cliffs rofe where yon gentle flopes

Mix with the vale; and fluctuating waves

Spread wide, where that rich vale with golden flowers

Shines; and where yonder winding chryftal rill

Slides thro' its fmooth fhorn margin, to the brink

Of Chadwell's azure pool. From Chadwell's pool

To London's plains, the Cambrian artift brought

His ample aqueduct*; fuppos'd a work

* The New River brought from Chadwell, a fpring in the
meadows between Hertford and Ware, by Sir HUGH MIDDLE-
TON, a native of Wales.

Of

Of matchlefs fkill, by thofe who ne'er had heard

How, from Prenefte's heights and Anio's banks,

By Tivoli, to Rome's imperial walls,

On marble arches came the limpid ftore,

And out of jafper rocks in bright cafcades

With never ceafing murmur gufh'd; or how,

To Lufitanian Ulyfippo's towers *,

The filver current o'er Alcant'ra's vale

Roll'd high in air, as ancient poets feign'd

Eridanus to roll thro' Heaven : to thefe

Not fordid lucre, but the honeft wifh

Of future fame, or care for public weal,

Exiftence gave; and unconfin'd, as dew

Falls from the hand of Evening on the fields,

They flow'd for all. Our mercenary ftream,

No grandeur boafting, here obfcurely glides

O'er graffy lawns or under willow fhades.

As, thro' the human form, arterial tubes

* The ancient name of Lifbon.

Branch'd

Branch'd every way, minute and more minute,

The circulating fanguine fluid extend ;

So, pipes innumerable to peopled ftreets

Tranfmit the purchas'd wave. Old Lee, meanwhile,

Beneath his moffy grot o'erhung with boughs

Of poplar quivering in the breeze, furveys

With eye indignant his diminifh'd tide *

That laves yon ancient priory's wall †, and fhows

In its clear mirrour Ware's inverted roofs.

Ware once was known to Fame ; to her fair fields

Whilom the Gothic tournament's proud pomp

Brought Albion's valiant youth and blooming maids :

Pleas'd with ideas of the paft, the Mufe

* A confiderable part of the New River water is derived from the Lee, to the difadvantage of the navigation on that ftream.

† " About the 18th of Henry III. Margaret, Countefs of " Leicefter, and Lady of the Manor, founded a priory for friers " in the north part of this town of Ware, and dedicated the " fame to St. Francis." *Chauncy's Hertfordfhire.*

Bids

Bids Fancy's pencil paint the fcene, where they

In gilded barges on the glaffy ftream

Circled the reedy ifles, the fportive dance

Along the fmooth lawn led, or in the groves

Wander'd converfing, or reclin'd at eafe

To harmony of lutes and voices fweet

Refign'd the enchanted ear; till fudden heard

The filver trumpet's animating found

Summon'd the champions forth; on ftately fteeds,

In fplendid armour clad, the ponderous lance

With ftrenuous hand fuftaining, forth they came.

    Where gay pavilions rofe upon the plain,

Or azure awnings ftretch'd from tree to tree,

Mix'd with thick foliage, form'd a mimic fky

Of grateful fhade (as oft in Agra's ftreets

The filken canopy from fide to fide

Extends to break the fun's impetuous ray,

While monarchs pafs beneath); there fat the Fair,

A glittering train on coftly carpets rang'd,

A group

A group of beauties all in youthful prime,

Of various feature and of various grace!

The penfive languifh, and the fprightly air,

The engaging fmile, and all the namelefs charms

Which tranfient hope, or fear, or grief, or joy,

Wak'd in th' expreffive eye, th' enamour'd heart

Of each young hero rous'd to daring deeds.

Nor this aught ftrange, that thofe whom love infpir'd

Prov'd ev'ry means the lovely fex to pleafe:

This ftrange, indeed, how cuftom thus could teach

The tender breaft complacence in the fight

Of barb'rous fport, where friend from hand of friend

The fatal wound full oft receiv'd, and fell

A victim to falfe glory; as that day

Fell gallant PEMBROKE, while his pompous fhow

Ended in filent gloom*.   One pitying tear

To

* " In the 25th of Henry III. on the 27th of June, Gilbert
" Marfhal, Earl of Pembroke, a potent Peer of the Realm,
" proclaimed here [at Ware] a difport of running on horfeback
" with

To human frailty paid ; my roving fight

Purfues its pleafing courfe o'er neighb'ring hills,

Where frequent hedge-rows interfect rich fields

Of many a different form and different hue,

Bright with ripe corn, or green with grafs, or dark

With clover's purple bloom ; o'er Widbury's mount

With that fair crefcent crown'd of lofty elms,

Its own peculiar boaft.; and o'er the woods

That round immure the deep fequefter'd dale

Of Langley*, down whofe flow'r-embroider'd meads

" with lances, which was then called a tournament." *Chauncy's*
Hift. of Hertfordfhire.

" At this tournament, the faid Gilbert was flain by a fall
" from his horfe ; Robert de Say, one of his knights, was
" killed, and feveral others wounded." *Smollet's Hift. of
England.*

* This delightful retreat, commonly called Langley-bottom,
is fituated about half a mile from Ware, and the fame diftance
from Amwell. The fcene is adapted to contemplation, and
poffeffes fuch capabilities of improvement, that the genius of a
Shenftone might eafily convert it to a fecond Leafowes. The
tranfition from this folitude to Widbury-Hill, is made in a walk
of a few minutes, and the profpect from that hill, in a fine
evening, is beautiful beyond defcription.

Swift

Swift Afh thro' pebbly fhores meandering rolls,

Elyfian fcene! as from the living world

Secluded quite; for of that world, to him

Whofe wanderings trace thy winding length, appears

No mark, fave one white folitary fpire

At diftance rifing thro' the tufted trees—

Elyfian fcene! reclufe as that, fo fam'd

For folitude, by Warwick's ancient walls,

Where under umbrage of the moffy cliff

Victorious Guy, fo legends fay, reclin'd

His hoary head befide the filver ftream,

In meditation rapt——Elyfian fcene!

At evening often, while the fetting fun

On the green fummit of thy eaftern groves

Pour'd full his yellow radiance; while the voice

Of Zephyr whifpering midft the ruftling leaves,

The found of water murmuring thro' the fedge,

The turtle's plaintive call, and mufic foft

Of diftant bells, whofe ever varying notes

In

In flow fad meafure mov'd, combin'd to footh

The foul to fweet folemnity of thought;

Beneath thy branchy bowers of thickeft gloom,

Much on the imperfect ftate of Man I have mus'd:

How Pain o'er half his hours her iron reign

Ruthlefs extends; how Pleafure from the path

Of Innocence allures his fteps; how Hope

Directs his eye to diftant Joy, that flies

His fond purfuit; how Fear his fhuddering heart

Alarms with fancy'd ill; how Doubt and Care

Perplex his thought; how foon the tender rofe

Of Beauty fades, the fturdy oak of Strength

Declines to earth, and over all our pride

Stern Time triumphant ftands. From general fate

To private woes then oft has Memory pafs'd,

And mourn'd the lofs of many a friend belov'd;

Of thee, De Horne, kind, generous, wife, and
　　　good!

And thee, my Turner, who in vacant youth,

Here oft in converfe free, or ftudious fearch

　　　　　　　　　　　　　　　　　Of

Of claffic lore, accompanied my walk!

From Ware's green bowers, to Devon's myrtle vales,

Remov'd a while, with profpect opening fair

Of ufeful life and honour in his view;

As falls the vernal bloom before the breath

Of blafting Eurus, immature he fell!

The tidings reach'd my ear, and in my breaft,

Aching with recent wounds*, new anguifh wak'd.

When melancholy thus has chang'd to grief,

That grief in foft forgetfulnefs to lofe,

I have left the gloom for gayer fcenes, and fought

Thro' winding paths of venerable fhade,

The airy brow where that tall fpreading beech

O'er-tops furrounding groves, up rocky fteeps

Tree over tree difpos'd; or ftretching far

Their fhadowy coverts down th' indented fide

Of fair corn-fields; or pierc'd with funny glades,

That yield the cafual glimpfe of flowery meads

And fhining filver rills; on thefe the eye

* See Elegy written at Amwell, 1768, p. 49.

Then

Then wont to expatiate pleas'd ; or more remote

Survey'd yon vale of Lee, in verdant length

Of level lawn fpread out to Kent's blue hills,

And the proud range of glitt'ring fpires that rife

In mifty air on Thames's crowded fhores.

How beautiful, how various, is the view

Of thefe fweet paftoral landfcapes ! fair, perhaps,

As thofe renown'd of old, from Tabor's height,

Or Carmel feen ; or thofe, the pride of Greece,

Tempè or Arcady ; or thofe that grac'd

The banks of clear Elorus, or the fkirts

Of thymy Hybla, where Sicilia's ifle

Smiles on the azure main ; there once was heard

The Mufe's lofty lay.——How beautiful,

How various is yon view ! delicious hills

Bounding fmooth vales, fmooth vales by winding

    ftreams

Divided, that here glide thro' graffy banks

In

In open fun, there wander under fhade

Of afpen tall, or ancient elm, whofe boughs

O'erhang grey caftles, and romantic farms,

And humble cots of happy fhepherd fwains.

Delightful habitations! with the fong

Of birds melodious charm'd, and bleat of flocks

From upland paftures heard, and low of kine

Grazing the rufhy mead, and mingled founds

Of falling waters and of whifp'ring winds—

Delightful habitations! o'er the land

Difpers'd around, from Waltham's ofier'd ifles

To where bleak Nafing's lonely tower o'erlooks

Her verdant fields; from Raydon's pleafant groves

And Hunfdon's bowers on Stort's irriguous marge,

By Rhye's old walls, to Hodfdon's airy ftreet;

From Haly's woodland to the flow'ry meads

Of willow-fhaded Stanfted, and the flope

Of AMWELL's Mount, that crown'd with yellow corn

There from the green flat, foftly fwelling, fhows

Like

Like some bright vernal cloud by Zephyr's breath
Just rais'd above the horizon's azure bound.

As one long travell'd on Italia's plains,
The land of pomp and beauty, still his feet
On his own Albion joys to fix again;
So my pleas'd eye, which o'er the prospect wide
Has wander'd round, and various objects mark'd,
On AMWELL rests at last, its favourite scene!
How picturesque the view! where up the side
Of that steep bank, her roofs of russet thatch
Rise mix'd with trees, above whose swelling tops
Ascends the tall church tow'r, and loftier still
The hill's extended ridge. How picturesque!
Where flow beneath that bank the silver stream
Glides by the flowery isle, and willow groves
Wave on its northern verge, with trembling tufts
Of osier intermix'd. How picturesque
The slender group of airy elm, the clump

Of

Of pollard oak, or afh, with ivy brown

Entwin'd; the walnut's gloomy breadth of boughs,

The orchard's ancient fence of rugged pales,

The hayftack's dufky cone, the mofs-grown fhed,

The clay-built barn; the elder-fhaded cot,

Whofe white-wafh'd gable prominent thro' green

Of waving branches fhows, perchance infcrib'd

With fome paft owner's name, or rudely grac'd

With ruftic dial, that fcarcely ferves to mark

Time's ceafelefs flight; the wall with mantling vines

O'erfpread, the porch with climbing woodbine

     wreath'd,

And under fheltering eves the funny bench

Where brown hives range, whofe bufy tenants fill,

With drowfy hum, the little garden gay,

Whence blooming beans, and fpicy herbs, and flowers,

Exhale around a rich perfume! Here refts

The empty wain; there idle lies the plough:

By Summer's hand unharnefs'd, here the fteed,

                    Short

Short eafe enjoying, crops the daified lawn;

Here bleats the nurfling lamb, the heifer there

Waits at the yard-gate lowing. By the road,

Where the neat ale-houfe ftands (fo once ftood thine,

Deferted Auburn! in immortal fong

Confign'd to Fame*), the cottage fire recounts

The praife he earn'd, when crofs the field he drew

The ftraighteft furrow, or neateft built the rick,

Or led the reaper band in fultry noons

With unabating ftrength, or won the prize

At many a crowded wake. Befide her door,

The cottage matron whirls her circling wheel,

And jocund chants her lay. The cottage maid

Feeds from her loaded lap her mingled train

Of clamorous hungry fowls; or o'er the ftyle

Leaning with downcaft look, the artlefs tale

Of evening courtfhip hears. The fportive troop

* See The Deferted Village, a beautiful poem, by the late
Dr. Goldfmith.

Of cottage children on the graffy wafte

Mix in rude gambols, or the bounding ball

Circle from hand to hand, or ruftic notes

Wake on their pipes of jointed reed : while near

The careful fhepherd's frequent-falling ftrokes

Fix on the fallow lea his hurdled fold,

Such rural life ! fo calm, it little yields

Of interefting act, to fwell the page

Of hiftory or fong; yet much the foul

Its fweet fimplicity delights, and oft

From noife of bufy towns, to fields and groves,

The Mufe's fons have fled to find repofe.

Fam'd WALTON*, erft, the ingenious fifher fwain,

Oft our fair haunts explor'd; upon Lee's fhore,

* ISAAC WALTON, author of The Complete Angler, an ingenious biographer, and no defpicable poet. The fcene of his Anglers' Dialogues, is the Vale of Lee, between Tottenham and Ware; it feems to have been a place he much frequented : he particularly mentions Amwell-hill,

Beneath

Beneath fome green tree oft his angle laid,

His fport fufpending to admire their charms.

He, who in verfe his Country's ftory told*,

Here

***

* WILLIAM WARNER, author of Albion's England, an Hiftorical Poem; an epifode of which, intitled Argentile and Curan, has been frequently reprinted, and is much admired by the lovers of old Englifh Poetry. The ingenious Dr. PERCY, who has inferted this piece in his Collection, obferves that, " though Warner's name is fo feldom mentioned, his contem- " poraries ranked him on a level with Spenfer, and called them " the Homer and Virgil of their age;" that " Warner was " faid to have been a Warwickfhire man, and to have been " educated at Magdalen Hall; that, in the latter part of his " life, he was retained in the fervice of Henry Cary, Lord " Hunfdon, to whom he dedicates his poem; but that more of " his hiftory is not known." Mrs. COOPER, in her Mufes' Library, after highly applauding his poetry, adds, " What " were the circumftances and accidents of his life, we have " hardly light enough to conjecture; any more than, by his " dedication, it appears he was in the fervice of the Lord " Hunfdon, and acknowledges very gratefully both father and " fon for his patrons and benefactors."—By the following ex- tract from the Parifh Regifter of Amwell, it may be reafonably concluded, that Warner refided for fome time at that village; and, as his profeffion of an attorney is particularly mentioned, it is pretty evident, that, whatever dependence he might have on Lord Hunfdon, it could not be in the capacity of a menial

G   fervant.

Here dwelt awhile; perchance here sketch'd the scene,

Where his fair ARGENTILE, from crowded courts

For pride self-banish'd, in sequester'd shades

Sojourn'd disguis'd, and met the slighted youth

Who long had sought her love—the gentle bard

Sleeps here, by Fame forgotten ; (fickle Fame

Too oft forgets her favourites !) By his side

Sleeps gentle HASSAL *, who with tenderest care

Here

fervant.   Though Warner's merit, as a poet, may have been
too highly rated, it was really not inconsiderable ; his Argentile
and Curan has many beauties ; but it has also the faults common
to the compositions of his age, especially a most disgusting in-
delicacy of sentiment and expression.

" Ma. William Warner, a man of good yeares and honest
" reputation, by his profession an Atturney at the Common
" Please, Author of Albion's England ; dying soddenly in the
" night in his bedde, without any former complaynt or sick-
" nesse, on Thursday night beeing the 9th of March, was bu-
" ried the Saturday following, and lieth in the church at the
" upper end, under the stone of Gwalter Fader."

Parish Register of Amwell, 1608-9.

* THOMAS HASSAL, vicar of Amwell ; he kept the above-
mentioned Parish Register with uncommon care and precision,
enriching

Here watch'd his village charge; in nuptial bonds

Their hands oft join'd; oft heard, and oft reliev'd

Their little wants; oft heard and oft compos'd,

Sole arbiter, their little broils; oft urg'd

enriching it with many entertaining anecdotes of the parties
regiſtered. He performed his duty in the moſt hazardous cir-
cumſtances, it appearing that the plague twice raged in the
village during his reſidence there; in 1603 when 26 perſons,
and in 1625 when 22 perſons died of it, and were buried in his
church-yard. The character here given of him muſt be allowed,
ſtrictly ſpeaking, to be imaginary; but his compoſition, in the
ſaid regiſter, appeared to me to breathe ſuch a ſpirit of piety,
ſimplicity, and benevolence, that I almoſt think myſelf autho-
riſed to aſſert that it was his real one. He himſelf is regiſtered
by his ſon Edmund Haſſal, as follows :

" Thomas Haſſal, Vicar of this pariſh, where he had conti-
" nued reſident 57 years 7 months and 16 days, in the reigns
" of Queen Elizabeth, King James, and King Charles, de-
" parted this life September 24th, Thurſday, and was buried
" September 26th, Saturday. His body was laid in the chancel
" of this church, under the prieſts or marble ſtone. Ætatis 84.
" Non erat ante, nec erit poſt te ſimilis. *Edmund Haſſal.*"
Regiſter of Amwell, 1657.

Eliſabeth Haſſal, wife of the ſaid Thomas Haſſal, died about
the ſame time, aged 78 years 8 months, married 46 years and 4
months.

G 2
Their

Their flight from folly and from vice; and oft
Dropt on their graves the tear, to early worth
Or ancient friendſhip due. In dangerous days,
When Death's fell Fury, pale-eyed Peſtilence,
Glar'd horror round; his duty he diſcharg'd
Unterrified, unhurt; and here, at length,
Clos'd his calm inoffenſive uſeful life
In venerable age: her life with him
His faithful conſort clos'd; on earth's cold breaſt
Both ſunk to reſt together.——On the turf,
Whence Time's rude graſp has torn their ruſtic
            tombs,
I ſtrew freſh flowers, and make a moment's pauſe
Of ſolemn thought; then ſeek th' adjacent ſpot,
From which, thro' theſe broad lindens' verdant arch,
The ſteeple's Gothic wall and window dim
In perſpective appear; then homeward turn
By where the Muſe, enamour'd of our ſhades,
Deigns ſtill her favouring preſence; where my friend,

I   The

The Britiſh Tasso*, oft from buſy ſcenes
To rural calm and letter'd eaſe retires.

As ſome fond lover leaves his favourite nymph,

Oft looking back, and lingering in her view,

So now reluctant this retreat I leave,

Look after look indulging; on the right,

Up to yon airy battlement's broad top

Half veil'd with trees, that, from th' acclivious ſteep,

Jut like the pendent gardens, fam'd of old,

Beſide Euphrates' bank; then, on the left,

Down to thoſe ſhaded cots, and bright expanſe

Of water ſoftly ſliding by: once, where

That bright expanſe of water ſoftly ſlides,

O'erhung with ſhrubs that fring'd the chalky rock,

A little fount pour'd forth its gurgling rill,

In flinty channel trickling o'er the green,

From Emma nam'd; perhaps ſome ſainted maid,

* Mr. Hoole, Tranſlator of Taſſo's Jeruſalem Delivered.

For

For holy life rever'd ; to fuch, erewhile,

Fond Superftition many a pleafant grove,

And limpid fpring, was wont to confecrate.

Of EMMA's ftory nought Tradition fpeaks ;

Conjecture, who, behind Oblivion's veil,

Along the doubtful paft delights to ftray,

Boafts now, indeed, that from her well the place

Receiv'd its appellation *.——Thou, fweet Vill,

Farewell ! and ye, fweet fields, where Plenty's horn

Pours liberal boons, and Health propitious deigns

Her chearing fmile ! you not the parching air

Of arid fands, you not the vapours chill

Of humid fens, annoy ; Favonius' wing,

From off your thyme-banks and your trefoil meads,

---

* In Doomfday-book, this village of Amwell is written Em-
mevelle, perhaps originally Emma's well. When the New
River was opened, there was a fpring here which was taken into
that aqueduct. Chadwell, the other fource of that river, evi-
dently received its denomination from the tutelar Saint, St. Chad,
who feems to have given name to fprings and wells in different
parts of England.

Wafts

Wafts balmy redolence; robuſt and gay

Your ſwains induſtrious iſſue to their toil,

Till your rich glebe, or in your granaries ſtore

Its generous produce: annual ye reſound

The ploughman's ſong, as he thro' reeking ſoil

Guides ſlow his ſhining ſhare; ye annual hear

The ſhouts of harveſt, and the prattling train

Of chearful gleaners:—and th' alternate ſtrokes

Of loud flails echoing from your loaded barns,

The pallid Morn in dark November wake.

But, happy as ye are, in marks of wealth

And population; not for theſe, or aught

Beſide, wiſh I, in hyperbolic ſtrains

Of vain applauſe, to elevate your fame

Above all other ſcenes; for ſcenes as fair

Have charm'd my ſight, but tranſient was the view:

You, thro' all ſeaſons, in each varied hour

For obſervation happieſt, oft my ſteps

Have travers'd o'er; oft Fancy's eye has ſeen

Gay

Gay Spring trip lightly on your lovely lawns,

To wake freſh flowers at morn; and Summer ſpread

His liſtleſs limbs, at noon-tide, on the marge

Of ſmooth tranſlucent pools, where willows green

Gave ſhade, and breezes from the wild mint's bloom

Brought odour exquiſite; oft Fancy's ear,

Deep in the gloom of evening woods, has heard

The laſt ſad ſigh of Autumn, when his throne

To Winter he reſign'd; oft Fancy's thought,

In extaſy, where from the golden eaſt,

Or dazzling ſouth, or crimſon weſt, the Sun

A different luſtre o'er the landſcape threw,

Some Paradiſe has form'd, the blifsful ſeat

Of Innocence and Beauty! while I wiſh'd

The ſkill of CLAUDE, or RUBENS, or of Him

Whom now on Lavant's banks, in groves that
      breathe

Enthuſiaſm ſublime, the Siſter Nymphs *

     * Painting and Poetry.

                     Inſpire;

Infpire †; that, to the idea fair, my hand

Might permanence have lent !—Attachment ftrong

Springs from delight beftow'd ; to me delight

Long ye have given, and I have given you praife !

† Mr. GEORGE SMITH of Chichefter, a juftly celebrated Landfcape Painter, and alfo a Poet. Lavant is the name of the river at Chichefter, which city gave birth to the fublime COLLINS.

————— The gentle Bard
Sleeps here by Fame forgotten—

AMOEBAEAN

ECLOGUES.

ADVERTISEMENT.

Much of the Rural Imagery which our Country affords, has already been introduced in Poetry; but many obvious and pleasing appearances seem to have totally escaped notice. To describe these, is the business of the following Eclogues. The plan of the Carmen Amoebaeum, or Responsive Verse of the Antients, inconsistent as it may be deemed with modern manners, was preferred on this occasion, as admitting an arbitrary and desultory disposition of ideas, where it was found difficult to preserve a regular connection.

E C L O G U E   I.

RURAL SCENERY; or, The Describers.

DECEMBER's froſt had bound the fields and
    ſtreams,

And Noon's bright ſun effus'd its chearful beams:

Where woodland, northward, ſcreen'd a pleaſant plain,

And on dry fern-banks brouz'd the fleecy train,

Two gentle youths, whom rural ſcenes could pleaſe,

Both ſkill'd to frame the tuneful rhyme with eaſe,

Charm'd with the proſpect, ſlowly ſtray'd along,

Themſelves amuſing with alternate ſong.

FIRST.

FIRST.

Thefe pollard oaks their tawny leaves retain,
Thefe hardy hornbeams yet unftripp'd remain;
The wintry groves all elfe admit the view
Thro' naked ftems of many a varied hue.

SECOND.

Yon fhrubby flopes a pleafing mixture fhow;
There the rough elm and fmooth white privet grow,
Straight fhoots of afh with bark of gloffy grey,
Red cornel twigs, and maple's ruffet fpray.

FIRST.

Thefe ftony fteeps with fpreading mofs abound,
Grey on the trees, and green upon the ground;
With tangling brambles ivy interweaves,
And bright mezerion* fpreads its cluft'ring leaves.

SECOND.

* Mezerion, Laureola Sempervirens: *vulg*. Spurge-Laurel.
This beautiful little evergreen is frequent among our woods and
coppices. Its fmooth fhining leaves are placed on the top of the ftems

in

SECOND.

Old oaken ſtubs tough ſaplings there adorn,

There hedge-row plaſhes yield the knotty thorn;

The ſwain for different uſes theſe avail,

And form the traveller's ſtaff, the threſher's flail.

FIRST.

Where yon brown hazels pendent catkins bear,

And prickly furze unfolds its bloſſoms fair,

The vagrant artiſt oft at eaſe reclines,

And broom's green ſhoots in beſoms neat combines,

SECOND.

See, down the hill, along the ample glade,

The new-fallen wood in even ranges laid!

There his keen bill the buſy workman plies,

And bids in heaps his well-bound faggots riſe.

in circular tufts or cluſters. Its flowers are ſmall, of a light green, and perfume the air at a diſtance in an agreeable manner. It blows very early in mild ſeaſons and warm ſituations. The common deciduous Mezerion, frequently planted in gardens, though very different in appearance, is another ſpecies of this genus.

FIRST.

FIRST.

Soon ſhall kind Spring her flowery gifts beſtow;

On ſunny banks when ſilver ſnowdrops blow,

And tufts of primroſe all around are ſpread,

And purple violets all their fragrance ſhed.

SECOND.

The woods then white anemonies array,

And lofty ſallows their ſweet bloom diſplay,

And ſpicy hyacinths azure bells unfold,

And crowfoot clothes the mead with ſhining gold.

FIRST.

Then ſoon gay Summer brings his gaudy train,

His crimſon poppies deck the corn-clad plain;

There ſcabious blue *, and purple knapweed † riſe,

And weld ‡ and yarrow ſhow their various dyes.

---

* Scabious: Scabioſa Vulgaris.   † Knapweed: Jaꞯea
Vulgaris.   ‡ Weld: Luteola Vulgaris, or Dyers' Weed.
——Theſe plants, with many others not inferior in beauty, are
frequent on the balks, or ridges, which ſeparate different kinds
of corn in our common fields.

SECOND.

SECOND.

In fhady lanes red foxglove bells appear,
And golden fpikes the downy mulleins rear *;
Th' inclofure ditch luxuriant mallows hide,
And branchy fuccory crowds the pathway fide.

FIRST.

Th' autumnal fields few pleafing plants fupply,
Save where pale eyebright grows in paftures
    dry,
Or vervain blue, for magic rites renown'd,
And in the village precincts only found †.

---

* The Digitalis, or Foxglove, is a very beautiful plant; there are feveral varieties of it which are honoured with a place in our gardens. The Mullein is not inferior in beauty, confequently merits equal notice.

† It is a vulgar opinion, that Vervain never grows in any place more than a quarter of a mile diftant from a houfe.—Vide Miller's Gardener's Dictionary, article Verbena.

SECOND.

Th' autumnal hedges withering leaves embrown,
Save where wild climbers ſpread their ſilvery down *
And rugged blackthorns bend with purple ſloes,
And the green ſkewerwood feeds of ſcarlet ſhows †.

FIRST.

When healthful ſallads crown the board in ſpring,
And nymphs green parſley from the gardens bring,
Mark well leſt hemlock mix its poiſonous leaves—
Their ſemblance oft th' incautious eye deceives.

* Wild Climbers: Clematis, Viorna, or, Traveller's Joy. The white downy feeds of this plant make a very conſpicuous figure on our hedges in autumn.

† Skewerwood: Evonymus; or, Spindle-tree. The twigs of this ſhrub are of a fine green; the capſules, or feed-veſſels, of a fine purple; and the feeds of a rich ſcarlet. In autumn, when the capſules open and ſhew the feeds, the plant has a moſt beautiful appearance.

SECOND.

SECOND.

Warn, O ye Shepherds ! warn the youth who play
On hamlet waftes, befide the public way ;
There oft rank foils pernicious plants produce,
There nightfhade's berry fwells with deadly juice,

FIRST.

What varied fcenes this pleafant country yields,
Form'd by th' arrangement fair of woods and fields !
On a green hillock, by the fhady road,
My dwelling ftands—a fweet reclufe abode !
And o'er my darken'd cafement intertwine
The fragrant briar, the woodbine, and the vine.

SECOND.

How different fcenes our different taftes delight !
Some feek the hills, and fome the vales invite.
Where o'er the brook's moift margin hazels meet,
Stands my lone home—a pleafant, cool retreat !

Gay loofeſtrife there and pale valerian ſpring *,
And tuneful reed-birds midſt the ſedges ſing.

FIRST.

Before my door the box-edg'd border lies,
Where flowers of mint and thyme and tanſy riſe;
Along my wall the yellow ſtonecrop grows,
And the red houſeleek on my brown thatch blows.

SECOND.

Among green oſiers winds my ſtream away,
Where the blue halcyon ſkims from ſpray to
ſpray,
Where waves the bulruſh as the waters glide,
And yellow flag-flow'rs deck the funny ſide.

* Loofeſtrife: Lyſimachia Lutea Vulgaris. Dr. Hill obſerves,
that it is ſo beautiful a plant, in its erect ſtature, regular
growth, and elegant flowers, that it is every way worthy to be
taken into our gardens. It is frequent in moiſt places. The
flowers are of a bright gold colour.

FIRST.

FIRST.

Spread o'er the flope of yon fteep weftern hill,

My fruitful orchard fhelters all the vill;

There pear-trees tall their tops afpiring fhow,

And apple-boughs their branches mix below.

SECOND.

Eaft from my cottage ftretch delightful meads,

Where rows of willows rife, and banks of reeds;

There roll clear rivers; there, old elms between,

The mill's white roof and circling wheels are feen.

FIRST.

PALEMON's garden hawthorn hedges bound,

With flow'rs of white, or fruit of crimfon, crown'd;

There vernal lilacs fhow their purple bloom,

And fweet fyringas all the air perfume;

The fruitful mulberry fpreads its umbrage cool,

And the rough quince o'erhangs the little pool.

H 3   SECOND.

SECOND.

Albino's fence green currants hide from view,
With bunches hung of red or amber hue ;
Beside his arbour blows the jasmine fair,
And scarlet beans their gaudy blossoms bear ;
The lofty hollyhock there its spike displays,
And the broad sunflow'r shows its golden rays.

FIRST.

Where moss-grown pales a sunny spot inclos'd,
And pinks and lilies all their hues expos'd,
Beneath a porch, with mantling vines enwreath'd,
The morning breeze the charming Sylvia
    breath'd:
Not pink nor lily with her face could vie,
And, O how soft the languish of her eye !
I saw and lov'd; but lov'd, alas, in vain !
She check'd my passion with severe disdain.

SECOND.

SECOND.

When o'er the meads with vernal verdure gay
The village children wont at eve to ſtray,
I pluck'd freſh flowrets from the graſſy ground,
And their green ſtalks with bending ruſhes bound;
My wreaths, my noſegays, then my DELIA dreſt,
Crown'd her fair brow, or bloom'd upon her
      breaſt.
Young as I was, the pleaſing thought was mine,
One day, fond boy, that beauty will be thine!

FIRST.

Beſide his gate, beneath the lofty tree,
Old THYRSIS' well-known ſeat I vacant ſee;
There, while his prattling offspring round him
      play'd,
He oft to pleaſe them toys of oſiers made:
That ſeat his weight ſhall never more ſuſtain,
That offspring round him ne'er ſhall ſport again.

SECOND.

Yon lone church tow'r that overlooks the hills!—
The fight my foul full oft with forrow fills:
There DAMON lies;—in prime of youth he died!—
A ford unknown, by night he vent'rous tried:
In vain he ftruggled with the foaming wave;
No friendly arm, alas, was near to fave!

FIRST.

Ceafe, friend! and, homeward as we bend our way,
Remark the beauties of the clofing day;
See, tow'rds the weft, the redd'ning Sun declines,
And o'er the fields his level luftre fhines.

SECOND.

How that bright landfcape lures the eye to gaze,
Where with his beams the diftant windows blaze!
And the gilt vane, high on the fteeple fpire,
Glows in the air—a dazzling fpot of fire!

FIRST.

F I R S T.

Behind yon hill he now forſakes our ſight,

And yon tall beeches catch his lateſt light;

The hamlet ſmokes in amber wreaths ariſe;

White miſt, like water, on the valley lies.

S E C O N D.

Where yon chalk cliffs th' horizon eaſtward bound,

And ſpreading elms the ancient hall ſurround,

The moon's bright orb ariſes from the main,

And Night in ſilence holds her ſolemn reign.

E C L O G U E II.

RURAL BUSINESS; or, The Agriculturists,

MAY's lib'ral hand her fragrant bloom dif-
  clos'd,

And herds and flocks on graffy banks repos'd ;

Soft Evening gave to eafe the tranquil hour,

And Philomel's wild warblings fill'd the bow'r.

Where near the village rofe the elm-crown'd hill,

And white-leav'd afpins trembled o'er the rill,

Three rural Bards, the village youth among,

The pleafing lore of rural bufinefs fung.

FIRST.

The care of farms we fing—attend the ftrain—

What fkill, what toil, fhall beft procure you gain ;

7   How

How different culture different ground requires;
While Wealth rewards whom Induſtry inſpires.

SECOND.

When thy light land on ſcorching gravel lies,
And to the ſpringing blade ſupport denies;
Fix on the wintry tilth the frequent fold,
And mend with cooling marl or untried mould.

THIRD.

If thy ſtrong loam ſuperfluous wet retain,
Lead thro' thy fields the ſubterraneous drain,
And o'er the ſurface mellowing ſtores expand
Of fiery lime, or incoherent ſand.

FIRST.

In vacant corners, on the hamlet waſte,
The ample dunghill's ſteaming heap be plac'd;
There many a month fermenting to remain,
Ere thy ſlow team diſperſe it o'er the plain.

SECOND.

SECOND.

The prudent farmer all manure provides,

The mire of roads, the mould of hedge-row fides;

For him their mud the ftagnant ponds fupply;

For him their foil, the ftable and the fty.

THIRD.

For this the fwain, on Kennet's winding fhore,

Digs fulphurous peat along the fable moor;

For this, where Ocean bounds the ftormy ftrand,

They fetch dank fea-weed to the neighb'ring land.

FIRST.

Who barren heaths to tillage means to turn,

Muft, ere he plough, the greenfward pare and burn;

Where rife the fmoking hillocks o'er the field,

The faline afhes ufeful compoft yield.

SECOND.

Where fedge or rufhes rife on fpongy foils,

Or rampant mofs th' impoverifh'd herbage fpoils,

Corrofive

Corrofive foot with liberal hand beftow;

Th' improving pafture foon its ufe will fhow.

T H I R D.

Hertfordian fwains on airy hills explore

The chalk's white vein, a fertilizing ftore;

This, from deep pits in copious bafkets drawn,

Amends alike the arable and lawn.

F I R S T.

Who fpends too oft in indolence the day,

Soon fees his farm his bafe negled betray;

His ufelefs hedge-greens docks and nettles bear,

And the tough cammock clogs his fhining fhare*.

S E C O N D.

Thy weedy fallows let the plough pervade,

Till on the top th' inverted roots are laid;

---

* Cammock: Ononis, or Reftharrow. The roots of this troublefome plant are fo ftrong, that it is credibly afferted they will ftop a plough drawn by feveral horfes.

There

There left to wither in the noon-tide ray,

Or by the fpiky harrow clear'd away.

T H I R D.

When wheat's green ftem the ridge begins to

hide,

Let the fharp weedhook's frequent aid be tried,

Left thy fpoil'd crop at harveft thou bemoan,

With twitch and twining bindweed overgrown.

F I R S T.

Much will rank melilot thy grain difgrace,

And darnel, felleft of the weedy race:

T' extirpate thefe might care or coft avail,

T' extirpate thefe nor care nor coft fhould fail.

S E C O N D.

When the foul furrow fetid mayweed fills,

The weary reaper oft complains of ills;

As his keen fickle grides along the lands,

The acrid herbage oft corrodes his hands.

T H I R D.

THIRD.

Wield oft thy fcythe along the graffy layes,
Ere the rude thiftle its light down difplays;
Elfe that light down upon the breeze will fly,
And a new ftore of noxious plants fupply.

FIRST.

Would ye from tillage ample gains receive,
With change of crops th' exhaufted foil relieve;
Next purple clover let brown wheat be feen,
And bearded barley after turnips green.

SECOND.

Bid here dark peas or tangled vetches fpread,
There buckwheat's white flow'r faintly ting'd with
     red;
Bid here potatoes deep green ftems be born,
And yellow cole th' inclofure there adorn.

THIRD.

Here let tall rye or fragrant beans afcend,
Or oats their ample panicles extend;

There

There reft thy glebe, left fallow not in vain,
To feel the fummer's fun and winter's rain.

F I R S T.

The fkill'd in culture oft repay their toil
By choice of plants adapted to their foil;
The fpiky faintfoin beft on chalk fucceeds,
The lucern hates cold clays and moory meads.

S E C O N D.

Beft on loofe fands, where brakes and briars once rofe,
Its deep-fring'd leaves the yellow carrot fhows;
Beft on ftiff loam rough teafels* rear their heads,
And brown coriander's odorous umbel fpreads.

T H I R D.

On barren mountains, bleak with chilly air,
Forbidding pafturage or the ploughman's care,
Laburnum's boughs a beauteous bloom difclofe,
Or fpiry pines a gloomy grove compofe.

* Teafel: Dipfacus Sativus. This plant is cultivated, in many places, for the ufe of the woollen manufacture. There are large fields of it in Effex; where the Coriander is alfo grown.

FIRST.

FIRST.

On rufhy marfhes, rank with watry weeds,

Clothe the clear'd foil with groves of waving reeds;

Of them the gard'ner annual fences forms,

To fhield his tender plants from vernal ftorms.

SECOND.

Cantabrian hills the purple faffron fhow;

Blue fields of flax in Lincoln's fenland blow;

On Kent's rich plains, green hop-grounds fcent the

    gales;

And apple-groves deck Hereford's golden vales*.

THIRD.

Shelter'd by woods the weald of Suffex lies;

Her fmooth green downs fublime from Ocean rife:

That, fitteft foil fupplies for growth of grain;

Thefe, yield beft pafture for the fleecy train.

* There is a part of Herefordfhire, from its extraordinary fertility and pleafantnefs, ufually denominated The Golden Vale.

FIRST.

Say, friends! whoe'er his refidence might chufe,
Would thefe fweet fcenes of fylvan fhade refufe,
And feek the black wafte of the barren wold,
That yields no fhelter from the heat or cold?

SECOND.

Dull are flow Oufa's mift-exhaling plains,
Where long rank grafs the morning dew retains:
Who paftures there in Autumn's humid reign,
His flock from ficknefs hopes to fave in vain.

THIRD.

The bleak, flat, fedgy fhores of Effex fhun,
Where fog perpetual veils the winter fun;
Though flattering Fortune there invite thy ftay,
Thy health the purchafe of her fmiles muft pay.

FIRST.

When, harveft paft, thy ricks of yellow corn
Rife round the yard, and fcent the breeze of morn;

Rude

Rude Winter's rage with timely care to avert,
Let the fkill'd thatcher ply his ufeful art.

SECOND.

When thy ripe walnuts deck the gloffy fpray,
Ere pilfering rooks purloin them faft away,
Wield thy tough pole, and lafh the trees amain,
Till leaves and hufks the lawn beneath diftain.

THIRD.

When thy green orchards fraught with fruit appear,
Thy lofty ladder 'midft the boughs uprear;
Thy bafket's hook upon the branch fufpend,
And with the fragrant burden oft defcend.

FIRST.

Spread on the grafs, or pil'd in heaps, behold
The pearmain's red, the pippin's fpeckled gold;
There fhall the ruffet's auburn rind be feen,
The redftreak's ftripes, and nonpareil's bright green.

SECOND.

Thefe on dry ftraw, in airy chambers, lay,
Where windows clear admit the noon-tide ray;
They, fafe from frofts, thy table fhall fupply,
Frefh to the tafte, and pleafing to the eye.

THIRD.

When favouring feafons yield thee ftore to
 fpare,
The circling mill and cumbrous prefs prepare;
From copious vats, the well-fermented juice
Will fparkling beverage for thy board produce.

FIRST.

From red to black when bramble-berries change,
And boys for nuts the hazel copfes range,
On new-reap'd fields the thick ftrong ftubble mow,
And fafe in ftacks about thy homeftead ftow.

SECOND.

SECOND.

With purple fruit when elder-branches bend,

And their bright hues the hips and cornels blend,

Ere yet chill hoar froſt comes, or ſleety rain,

Sow with choice wheat the neatly furrow'd plain.

THIRD.

When clamorous fieldfares ſeek the frozen mead,

And lurking ſnipes by gurgling runnels feed;

Then 'midſt dry fodder let thy herds be found,

Where ſheltering ſheds the well-ſtor'd crib ſur-

round.

FIRST.

Though Winter reigns, our labours never fail:

Then all day long we hear the ſounding flail;

And oft the beetle's ſtrenuous ſtroke deſcends,

That knotty block-wood into billets rends.

I 3   SECOND.

S E C O N D.

Then in the barns in motion oft are feen
The ruftling corn-fan, and the wiry fcreen:
In facks the tafker meafures up his grain,
And loads for market on the fpacious wain.

T H I R D.

Th' inclofure fence then claims our timely care,
The ditch to deepen, and the bank repair;
The well-plafh'd hedge with frequent ftakes con-
    fine,
And o'er its top tough wyths of hazel twine.

F I R S T.

Where in the croft the ruffet hayrick ftands,
The dextrous binder twifts his fedgy bands,
Acrofs the ftack his fharp-edg'd engine guides,
And the hard mafs in many a trufs divides *.

---

* Hay is ufually cut with an oblong, triangular inftrument,
called a Cutting-knife.

SECOND.

When froft thy turnips fixes in the ground,
And hungry flocks for food ftand bleating round,
Let fturdy youths their pointed peckers ply,
Till the rais'd roots loofe on the furface lie,

THIRD.

When ftormy days conftrain to quit the field,
The houfe or barn may ufeful bufinefs yield;
There crooked fnaths* of flexile fallow make,
Or of tough afh the fork-ftale and the rake.

FIRST.

Full many a chance defeats the farmer's pains,
Full many a lofs diminifhes his gains;
Wet fpoils the feed, or frofts its growth o'er-
        power,
Beafts break the ftalk, and birds the grain devour.

* Snath, is the technical term for the handle of a fcythe.

I 4   SECOND,

S E C O N D.

While plenteous crops reward thy toil and care,

Thy liberal aid may Age and Sicknefs fhare !

Nor let the widow'd cottager deplore

Her firelefs hearth, her cupboard's fcanty ftore,

T H I R D.

The haughty lord, whom luft of gain infpires,

From man and beaft exceffive toil requires:

The generous mafter views with pitying eyes

Their lot fevere, and food and reft fupplies,

F I R S T.

Amid Achaia's ftreamy vales of old,

Of works and days th' Afcrean Paftor told:

Around him, curious, came the ruftic throng,

And wondering liften'd to th' informing fong.

S E C O N D.

Where fam'd Anapus' limpid waters ftray,

Sicilia's Poet tun'd his Doric lay;

8   While

While o'er his head the pine's dark foliage hung,
And at his feet the bubbling fountain fprung.

THIRD.

The Latian MARO fung, where Mincio's ftream
Through groves of ilex caft a filvery gleam;
While down green vallies ftray'd his fleecy flocks,
Or flept in fhadow of the moffy rocks.

FIRST.

Fair fame to him, the bard whofe fong difplays
Of rural arts the knowledge and the praife!
Rich as the field with ripen'd harveft white—
A fcene of profit mingled with delight!

SECOND.

As dewy cherries to the tafte in June,
As fhady lanes to travellers at noon,
To me fo welcome is the Shepherd's ftrain;
To kindred fpirits never fung in vain!

THIRD.

THIRD.

While lindens fweet and fpiky chefnuts blow,

While beech bears maft, on oaks while acorns

    grow;

So long fhall laft the Shepherd's tuneful rhyme,

And pleafe in every age and every clime!

ORIENTAL

ECLOGUES.

ADVERTISEMENT.

The ORIENTAL ECLOGUES of COLLINS have such excellence, that it may be suppofed they muft preclude the appearance of any fubfequent Work with the fame title. This confideration did not efcape the Author of the following Poems; but, as the fcenery and fentiment of his Predeceffor were totally different from his own, he thought it matter of little confequence.

This kind of compofition is, in general, fubject to one difadvantage, for which allowance fhould be made. He, who defcribes what he has feen, may defcribe correctly: he, who defcribes what he has not feen, muft depend for much on the accounts of others, and fupply the reft from his own imagination.

6

Stothard del.   Heath sculp.

Z E R A D ;

OR,

THE ABSENT LOVER;

AN ARABIAN ECLOGUE,

THE learned and ingenious Mr. Jones, in his elegant and judicious Effay on Oriental Poetry, fpeaking of the Arabians, has the following paffage : " It fometimes happens," fays he, " that the young men of one tribe are in love with " the damfels of another ; and, as the tents are fre- " quently removed on a fudden, the lovers are often fepa- " rated in the progrefs of the courtfhip. Hence, almoft all " the Arabic poems open in this manner : The author be- " wails the fudden departure of his miftrefs, Hinda, Maia, " Zeineb, or Azza, and defcribes her beauty ; comparing " her to a wanton fawn that plays among the aromatic " fhrubs. His friends endeavour to comfort him ; but he " refufes confolation ; he declares his refolution of vifiting " his beloved, though the way to her tribe lie through a " dreadful wildernefs, or even through a den of lions."— The Author of the following Eclogue was ftruck with this outline, and has attempted to fill it up. An apology for expatiating on the pleafing fubjects of Love and Beauty, when nothing is faid to offend the ear of Chaftity, he fuppofes needlefs. If any, however, there be, who quef- tion the utility of at all defcribing thofe fubjects ; fuch may remember, that there is an Eaftern Poem, generally efteem- ed *facred*, which abounds with the moft ardent expreffions of the one, and luxuriant pictures of the other.

ZERAD; or, The ABSENT LOVER:

An ARABIAN Eclogue.

K ORASA's Tribe, a frequent-wandering train,
From Zenan's paſtures ſought Negiran's plain.
With them SEMIRA left her favourite ſhades,
The lovelieſt nymph of Yemen's ſportive maids !
Her parting hand her fair companions preſt ;
A tranſient ſorrow touch'd each tender breaſt ;
As ſome thin cloud acroſs the morning ray
Caſts one ſhort moment's gloom, and glides away :
Their cares, their ſports, they haſted ſoon to tend,
And loſt in them the memory of their friend.

But

But gallant ZERAD ill her abſence bore,—

A wealthy Emir from Katara's ſhore;

A warrior he, the braveſt of his race;

A bard high-honoured in his native place;

Age oft learn'd knowledge from his tuneful tongue,

And liſtening Beauty languiſh'd while he ſung.

What time the tribes in camp contiguous lay,

Oft with the Fair-one he was wont to ſtray;

There oft for her freſh fruits and flow'rs he
  ſought,

And oft her flocks to chryſtal fountains brought.

Where the tall palm-grove grac'd Alzobah's green,

And ſable tents in many a rank were ſeen*;

While Evening's ſteps the ſetting Sun purſued,

And the ſtill fields her balmy tears bedew'd;

The penſive Lover, there reclin'd apart,

Indulg'd the ſorrows of his anxious heart.

* The Arabian Tents are black. Vide Canticles, i. 5.

His

His graceful head the coftly turban dreft ;

The crimfon fafh confin'd his azure veft ;

His hand the founding arabeb* fuftain'd ;

And thus his voice in melody complain'd—

Soft as the night-bird's amorous mufic flows,

In Zibet's gardens, when fhe woos the rofe† :

‘ Bright ftar of Sora's fky, whofe matchlefs
  ‘ blaze

‘ Gilds thy proud tribe with mild, benignant rays !

‘ Sweet flow'r of Azem's vale, whofe matchlefs
  ‘ bloom

‘ O'er thy fam'd houfe fpreads exquifite perfume !

‘ Blithe fawn of Kofa, at the break of dawn,

‘ Midft groves of caffia, fporting on the lawn !

* Arabebbah, an Arabian and Moorifh inftrument of mufic. Vide Shaw's Travels, and Ruffell's Hiftory of Aleppo.

† Alluding to an Eaftern fable of the Nightingale courting the Rofe.

     ‘ Too

' Too charming Beauty! why muſt I bemoan

' Thee from my preſence thus abruptly flown?

' Ere the ſhrill trump to march the ſignal gave,

' And banners high in air began to wave;

' Ere the tall camel felt his wonted load,

' And herds and flocks ſlow mov'd along the road;

' Ere ſlow behind them march'd the warrior train,

' And the ſtruck tents left vacant all the plain;

' Could no fond plea obtain a longer ſtay?

' Would no kind hand th' intelligence convey?

' Ah, hapleſs me! to Aden's port I ſtray'd,

' Sought gold and gems, but loſt my lovely maid!

' My friends, they come my ſorrows to allay—

' Azor the wiſe, and Soliman the gay—

' One cries, " Let Reaſon hold her ſober reign,

" Nor Love's light trifles give thy boſom pain!

" For thee kind Science all her lore diſplays,

" And Fame awaits thee with the wreath of

" praiſe."

" O why,"

" O why," cries one, " is she alone thy care?

" She's fair, indeed, but other maids are fair:

" Negima's eyes with dazzling lustre shine,

" And her black tresses curl like Zebid's vine;

" On Hinda's brow Kushemon's lily blows,

" And on her cheek unfolds Nishapor's rose!

" With them, the tale, the song, the dance shall
  " please,

" When Mirth's free banquet fills the bow'r of
  " ease."

' Ah cease, said I; of love he little knows,

' Who with sage counsel hopes to cure its woes!

' Go, bid in air Yamama's lightnings stay,

' Or Perath's lion quit his trembling prey:

' Kind Science' lore with Beauty best we share,

' And Beauty's hands Fame's fairest wreaths pre-
  ' pare.

' I praise Negima's lovely hair and eyes;

' Nor Hinda's lily, nor her rose despise:

K 2

' But

' But Omman's pearls diffuse a brighter beam
' Than the gay pebbles of Kalafa's stream.—

 ' O lov'd Semira! whither doft thou rove?
' Tread thy soft steps by Sada's jasmine grove?
' Doft thou thy flocks on Ocah's mountain keep?
' Do Ared's olives whisper o'er thy sleep?—

' Ah, no!——the maid, perhaps, remote from
  ' these,
' Some hostile troop, in ambush laid, may seize:
' Too lovely captive! she, in triumph borne,
' The proud Pacha's throng'd haram shall adorn.

' Vain fear! around her march her valiant
  ' friends;
' Brave Omar's hand the bow of Ishmael bends;
' Strong Hassan's arm Kaaba's spear can wield,
' And rear on high El-makin's ponderous shield!

' Ah, shame to me! shall Sloth's dishonouring
  ' chain
' From love, from glory, Zerad here detain,

        ' Till

‘ Till grief my cheek with fickly faffron fpread,

‘ And my eyes, weeping, match th’ Argavan’s

   ‘ red * ?

‘ Hafte, bring my fteed, fupreme in ftrength and

   ‘ grace,

‘ Firft in the fight, and fleeteft in the chace;

‘ His fire renown’d on Gebel’s hills was bred,

‘ His beauteous dam in Derar’s paftures fed :

‘ Bring my ftrong lance that, ne’er impell’d in vain,

‘ Pierc’d the fierce tyger on Hegefa’s plain.

‘ Acrofs the Defart I her fteps purfue;

‘ Toil at my fide, and Danger in my view !

‘ There Thirft, fell dæmon ! haunts the fultry air,

‘ And his wild eye-balls roll with horrid glare;

* D’ Herbelot informs us, that Saffron Faces, and Argavan Eyes, are expreffions commonly ufed in the Eaft, to defcribe paffionate lovers, whofe melancholy appears in their countenances, and whofe eyes become red with weeping. The Argavan is fuppofed to be the Arbor Judæ; whofe bloffoms are of a bright purple. Vide Harmer’s Commentary on Solomon’s Song, page 162.

     ‘ There

‘ There deadly Sumiel*, ſtriding o’er the land,

‘ Sweeps his red wing, and whirls the burning
        ‘ ſand ;

‘ As winds the weary caravan along,

‘ The fiery ſtorm involves the hapleſs throng,

‘ I go, I go, nor Toil nor Danger heed ;

‘ The faithful lover Safety’s hand ſhall lead.

‘ The heart that foſters Virtue’s generous flames,

‘ Our Holy Prophet’s ſure protećtion claims.

    ‘ Delightful Irem† (midſt the lonely waſte

‘ By SHEDAD’s hand the paradiſe was plac’d)

‘ Each ſhady tree of varied foliage ſhows,

‘ And every flower and every fruit beſtows ;

---

* Sumiel : The fiery blaſting wind of the Deſart.

† “ Mahommed, in his Alcoran, in the Chapter of the
“ Morning, mentions a garden, called Irem, which is no leſs
“ celebrated by the Aſiatic poëts, than that of the Heſperides
“ by the Greeks. It was planted, as the Commentators ſay,
“ by a king, named SHEDAD ; and was once ſeen by an Ara-
“ bian, who wandered far into the Deſart, in ſearch of a loſt
“ camel.”   Jones’s Eſſay on Oriental Poetry.

                                    ‘ There

' There drop rich gums of every high perfume;

' There fing fweet birds of every gaudy plume;

' There foft-eyed Houries tread th' enamell'd

' green—

' Once, and no more, the happy feat was feen;

' As his ftray'd camel midft the wild he fought,

' Chance to the fpot the wandering ESAR brought;

' A blifsful Irem, 'midft the Defart drear,

' SEMIRA's tent my love-fick fight fhall chear.

' What palm of beauty tow'rs on Keran's hills?

' What myrrh with fragrance Sala's valley fills?

' 'Tis fhe, who left fo late her favourite fhades,

' The lovelieft nymph of Yemen's fportive maids!

' Look from thy tent, the curtains fair unfold,

' Give to my view thy veil of filk and gold;

' O lift that veil! thy radiant eyes difplay—

' Thofe radiant eyes fhall light me on my way!

' On Hejar's wild rocks from the Perfian main,

' Thus the Moon rifing lights the wilder'd fwain.

K 4   ' O raife

' O raife thy voice! the found fhall give delight,

' Like fongs of pilgrims diftant heard by night!

' I come, I come!'——He fpoke, and feiz'd the rein,

And his fleet courfer fpurn'd the fandy plain,

S E R I M;

OR,

THE ARTIFICIAL FAMINE.

AN EAST-INDIAN ECLOGUE.

THE following account of Britiſh conduct and its conſequences, in Bengal and the adjacent provinces, ſome years ago, will afford a ſufficient idea of the ſubject of the following Eclogue. After deſcribing the monopoly of ſalt, betel-nut, and tobacco, the Hiſtorian thus proceeds : " Mo-" ney, in this current, came but by drops ; it could not " quench the thirſt of thoſe who waited in India to receive " it. An expedient, ſuch as it was, remained to quicken " its pace.—The natives could live with little ſalt, but not " without food. Some of the agents ſaw themſelves well " ſituated for collecting the rice into ſtores ; they did ſo. " They knew the Gentoos would rather die, than violate " the precepts of their religion by eating fleſh. The alter-" native would therefore be, between giving what they had, " and dying. The inhabitants ſunk ; they that cultivated " the land, and ſaw the harveſt at the diſpoſal of others, " planted in doubt ; ſcarcity enſued ; then the monopoly " was eaſier managed. The people took to roots, and food " they had been unaccuſtomed to eat. Sickneſs enſued. In " ſome diſtricts, the languid Living left the bodies of their " numerous Dead unburied."——Short Hiſtory of Engliſh Tranſactions in the Eaſt-Indies, p. 145.

The above quotation ſufficiently proves, that the general plan of the following Poem is founded on fact. And, even with regard to its particlar incidents, there can be little doubt, but that, among the varied miſeries of millions, every picture of diſtreſs, which the Author has drawn, had its original.

SERIM; or, The Artificial Famine:

An East-Indian Eclogue.

―――――――――

' O Guardian Genius of this sacred wave*!
    ' O save thy sons, if thine the power to save!'
So SERIM spoke, as sad on Ganges' shore
He sat, his country's miseries to deplore—
' O Guardian Genius of this sacred wave!
' O save thy sons, if thine the power to save!
' From Agra's tow'rs to Muxadabat's † walls,
' On thee for aid the suffering Hindoo calls:

---

* The Hindoos worship a God or Genius of the Ganges.

† Muxadabat, or Morshedabat, a large city of India, about
two hundred miles above Calcutta. The name is commonly
pronounced with the accent on the last syllable: Muxadabàt.
I have taken the liberty to accommodate this, and some few
other words, to my verse, by altering the accentuation; a mat-
ter, I apprehend, of little consequence to the English reader.

                         ' Europe's

' Europe's fell race controul the wide domain,

' Engrofs the harveft, and enflave the fwain.

' Why rife thefe cumbrous piles along thy tide ?

' They hold the plenty to our prayers denied !

' Guards at their gates perpetual watch maintain,

' Where Want in anguifh craves relief in vain.

" Bring gold, bring gems," the infatiate plunderers
    cry ;

" Who hoards his wealth by Hunger's rage fhall
    " die."

' Ye Fiends ! ye have ravifh'd all our little ftore ;

' Ye fee we perifh, yet ye afk for more !

' Go ye yourfelves, and fearch for gold the mine ;

' Go, dive where pearls beneath the ocean fhine !

' What right have ye to plague our peaceful land ?

' No fhips of ours e'er fought your weftern ftrand :

' Ne'er from your fields we fnatch'd their crops
    ' away,

' Nor made your daughters or your fons our prey.

                         ' Not

‘ Not ev'n in thought we quit our native place—

‘ A calm, contented, inoffenfive race !

‘ By Avarice led, ye range remoteſt climes,

‘ And every nation execrates your crimes.

 ‘ When TIMUR's Houſe* renown'd, in Delhi
  ‘ reign'd,

‘ Diſtreſs, affiſtance unimplor'd obtain'd :

‘ When Famine o'er the afflicted region frown'd,

‘ And Sickneſs languiſh'd on the barren ground,

‘ The Imperial granaries wide diſplay'd their doors,

‘ And ſhips proviſion brought from diſtant ſhores;

‘ The laden camels crowded Kurah's vales,

‘ From Colgon's cliffs they hail'd the coming ſails.

---

* The famous Mahometan tyrant, Auranzebe, during a fa-
mine which prevailed in different parts of India, exerted himſelf
to alleviate the diſtreſs of his ſubjects. “ He remitted the taxes
“ that were due; he employed thoſe already collected in the
“ purchaſe of corn, which was diſtributed among the poorer
“ ſort. He even expended immenſe ſums out of the treaſury,
“ in conveying grain, by land and water, into the interior
“ provinces, from Bengal, and the countries which lie on the
“ five branches of the Indus.” Dow's Indoſtan, vol. iii. p. 340.

7

‘ But

‘ But ye !—even now, while fav’ring feafons fmile,

‘ And the rich glebe would recompenfe our toil,

‘ Dearth and Difeafe to you alone we owe;

‘ Ye caufe the mifchief, and enjoy the woe !

   ‘ This beauteous clime, but late, what plenty

      ‘ bleft !

‘ What days of pleafure, and what nights of reft !

‘ From. Gola’s ftreets, fam’d mart of fragrant

      ‘ grain !

‘ Trade’s chearful voice refounded o’er the plain;

‘ There now fad Silence liftens to the waves

‘ That break in murmurs round the rocky caves.

‘ Sweet were the fongs o’er Jumal’s level borne,

‘ While bufy thoufands throng’d to plant the corn;

‘ Now tenfold tax the farmer forc’d to yield,

‘ Defpairs, and leaves unoccupied the field.

‘ Sweet were the fongs of Burdwan’s mulberry

      ‘ grove,

‘ While the rich filk the rapid fhuttle wove;

                       ‘ Now

‘ Now from the loom our coftly veftments

  ‘ torn,

‘ The infulting robbers meaneft flaves adorn.

‘ In Malda’s fhades, on Purna’s palmy plain,

‘ The haplefs artifts, urg’d to toil in vain,

‘ Quit their fad homes, and mourn along the

  ‘ land,

‘ A penfive, pallid, felf-difabled band * !—

 ‘ The year revolves—“ Bring choiceft fruits and

   “ flowers !

 “ Spread wide the board in confecrated bowers ;

---

* “ Thofe who now made the things the Englifh moft want-
“ ed, were preffed on all fides—by their own neceffities, their
“ neighbours, and the agents employed to procure the Com-
“ pany’s inveftments, as the goods fent to Europe are called.
“ Thefe importunities were united, and urged fo much, fo
“ often, and in fuch ways, as to produce, among the people in
‘ the filk bufinefs, inftances of their cutting off their thumbs,
“ that the want of them might excufe them from following
‘ their trade, and the inconveniences to which they were ex-
“ pofed beyond the common lot of their neighbours.”

  Hiftory of Englifh Tranfactions in the Eaft-Indies.

         “ Bring

" Bring Joy, bring Sport, the song, the dance prepare!

" 'Tis DRUGAH's † Feaft, and all our friends muft

    " fhare !"

' The year revolves—nor fruits nor flowers are feen;

' Nor feftive board in bowers of holy green;

' Nor Joy, nor Sport, nor dance, nor tuneful ftrain:

' 'Tis DRUGAH's feaft—but Grief and Terror reign.

' Yet there, ingrate! oft welcome guefts ye came,

' And talk'd of Honour's laws and Friendfhip's flame.

  ' The year revolves—and BISHEN's * Faft invites

' On Ganges' marge to pay the folemn rites;

                    ' All,

---

† DRUGAH; a Hindoo Goddefs. "Drugah Poojah is the " grand general feaft of the Gentoos, ufually vifited by all " Europeans (by invitation), who are treated by the proprietors " of the feaft with the fruits and flowers in feafon, and are " entertained every evening with bands of fingers and dancers."

Vide Holwell's Indoftan, vol. ii.

* BISHEN, BISTNOO, or JAGGERNAUT, is one of the prin- cipal Hindoo deities. "This faft, dedicated to him, is called " the Sinan Jattra, or general wafhing in the Ganges; " and it is almoft incredible to think the immenfe multi-

                    " tude,

' All, boons of BISHEN, great Preferver, crave;

' All, in the facred flood, their bodies lave:

' No more, alas !—the multitude no more

' Bathe in the tide, or kneel upon the fhore;

' No more from towns and villages they throng,

' Wide o'er the fields, the public paths along:

' Sad on our ways, by human foot unworn,

' Stalks the dim form of Solitude forlorn !—

' From Ava's mountains Morn's bright eyes furvey

' Fair Ganges' ftreams in many a winding ftray :

' There fleecy flocks on many an ifland feed;

' There herds unnumber'd pafture many a mead;

' (While noxious herbs our laft refource fupply,

' And, dearth efcaping, by difeafe we die)

" Take thefe," ye cry, " nor more for food complain;

" Take thefe, and flay like us, and riot on the

      " flain !"

" tude, of every age and fex, that appears on both fides the
" river, throughout its whole courfe, at one and the fame
" time."   Vide Mr. Holwell, vol. ii. p. 124. 128.

            L   ' Ah

' Ah no! our Law the crime abhorr'd withstands;

' We die—but blood shall ne'er pollute our hands.

' O Guardian Genius of this sacred wave!

' Save, save thy sons, if thine the power to save!'

So SERIM spoke—while by the moon's pale beam,

The frequent corse came floating down the stream *.

He sigh'd, and rising turn'd his steps to rove

Where wav'd o'er Nizim's vale the coco-grove;

There, 'midst scorch'd ruins, one lone roof remain'd,

And one forlorn inhabitant contain'd.

The sound of feet he near his threshold heard;

Slow from the ground his languid limbs he rear'd:

' Come, Tyrant, come! perform a generous part,

' Lift thy keen steel, and pierce this fainting heart!

' Com'st thou for gold? my gold, alas, I gave,

' My darling daughter in distress to save!

* The Hindoos frequently cast the bodies of their deceased into the Ganges; with the idea, I suppose, of committing them to the disposal of the God or Genius of the River.

3   ' Thy

‘ Thy faithlefs brethren took the fhining ftore,

‘ Then from my arms the trembling virgin tore !

‘ Three days, three nights, I've languifh'd here

‘ alone—

‘ Three foodlefs days, three nights to fleep unknown!

‘ Come, Tyrant, come ! perform a generous part,

‘ Lift thy keen fteel, and pierce this fainting heart !'

" No hoftile fteps the haunt of Woe invade,"

Serim replied—and, paffing where the glade

A length of profpect down the vale difplay'd,

Another fight of mifery met his view ;

Another mournful voice his notice drew !

There, near a temple's recent ruin, ftood

A white-rob'd Bramin, by the facred flood :

His wives, his children, dead befide him lay—

Of Hunger thefe, and thofe of Grief the prey !

Thrice he with duft defil'd his aged head ;

Thrice o'er the ftream his hands uplifted fpread :

‘ Hear,

‘ Hear, all ye Powers to whom we bend in prayer!

‘ Hear, all who rule o'er water, earth, and air!

‘ 'Tis not for them, tho' lifeless there they lie;

‘ 'Tis not for me, tho' innocent I die;—

‘ My Country's breast the tyger, Avarice, rends,

‘ And loud to you her parting groan ascends.

‘ Hear, all ye Powers to whom we bend in prayer!

‘ Hear, all who rule o'er water, earth, and air!

‘ Hear, and avenge!——

‘ But hark! what voice, from yonder starry sphere,

‘ Slides, like the breeze of Evening, o'er my

‘ ear?

‘ Lo, BIRMAH's* form! on amber clouds enthron'd;

‘ His azure robe with lucid emerald zon'd;

* BIRMAH is a principal Deity of the Hindoos, in whose person they worship the divine attribute of Wisdom. From the best accounts we have of India, the intelligent part of the natives do not worship “ stocks and stones,” merely as such; but rather the Supreme Existence, in a variety of attributes or manifestations.

‘ He

' He looks celeſtial dignity and grace,

' And views with pity wretched human race!'

  " Forbear, raſh man! nor curſe thy country's foes;

  " Frail man to man forgivenefs ever owes.

  " When MOISASOOR * the fell to Earth's fair plain

  " Brought his deteſted offspring, Strife and Pain;

  " Revenge with them, relentlefs Fury, came,

  " Her boſom burning with infernal flame!

  " Her hair ſheds horror, like the comet's blaze;

  " Her eyes, all ghaſtly, blaſt where'er they gaze;

  " Her lifted arm a poiſon'd crice† ſuſtains;

  " Her garments drop with blood of kindred veins!

  " Who aſks her aid, muſt own her endlefs reign,

  " Feel her keen ſcourge, and drag her galling

      " chain!"

  ' The ſtrains ſublime in ſweeteſt muſic cloſe,

  ' And all the tumult of my ſoul compoſe.

* MOISASOOR : the Hindoo Author of Evil, ſimilar to our Satan.

† Crice, an Indian dagger.

' Yet

' Yet you, ye oppreſſors ! uninvok'd on you*,

' Your ſteps, the ſteps of Juſtice will purſue !

' Go, ſpread your white ſails on the azure main ;

' Fraught with our ſpoils, your native land regain ;

' Go, plant the grove, and bid the lake expand,

' And on green hills the pompous palace ſtand :

' Let Luxury's hand adorn the gaudy room,

' Smooth the ſoft couch, and ſhed the rich perfume—

' There Night's kind calm in vain ſhall ſleep invite,

' While fancied omens warn, and ſpectres fright :

' Sad ſounds ſhall iſſue from your guilty walls,

' The widow'd wife's, the ſonleſs mother's calls ;

' And infant Rajahs' bleeding forms ſhall riſe,

' And lift to you their ſupplicating eyes :

* The Reader muſt readily perceive the propriety of this turn of thought, in a Poem deſigned to have a moral tendency. There is much difference between a perſon wiſhing evil to his enemy, and preſaging that evil will be the conſequence of that enemy's crimes. The firſt is an immoral act of the will ; the ſecond, a neutral act of the judgment.

' Remorſe

' Remorfe intolerable your hearts will feel,

' And your own hands plunge deep the avenging

  fteel †.

' (For Europe's cowards Heaven's command difdain,

' To Death's cold arms they fly for eafe in vain.)

' For us, each painful tranfmigration o'er,

' Sweet fields receive us to refign no more ;

' Where Safety's fence for ever round us grows,

' And Peace, fair flower, with bloom unfading blows;

' Light's Sun unfetting fhines with chearing beam ;

' And Pleafure's River rolls its golden ftream !'

Enrapt he fpoke—then ceas'd the lofty ftrain,

And Orel's rocks return'd the found again.—

† The Hindoo religion ftrongly prohibits fuicide. Mr. Hol-
well gives us the following paffage from the Shaftah : " Who-
" foever, of the delinquent Debtah, fhall dare to free himfelf
" from the mortal form wherewith I fhall inclofe him ; thou,
" Sieb, fhalt plunge him into the Onderah for ever : he fhall
" not again have the benefit of the fifteen Boboons of purga-
" tion, probation, and purification."

A Britiſh ruffian, near in ambuſh laid,

Ruſh'd ſudden from the cane-iſle's ſecret ſhade ;

' Go to thy Gods !' with rage infernal cried,

And headlong plung'd the hapleſs Sage into the

foaming tide.

L I - P O;

OR,

THE GOOD GOVERNOR:

A CHINESE ECLOGUE.

THOSE who are converfant in the beſt accounts of China, particularly Du Halde's Hiſtory, muſt have remarked, that the Chineſe government, though arbitrary, is well regulated and mild ; and that a prince, in that country, can acquire no glory, but by attention to the welfare of his ſubjeƈts.   On this general idea is founded the plan of the following Poem.

LI-PO; or, The Good Governor:
A Chinese Eclogue.

WHERE Honan's hills Kianfi's vale inclofe,

 And Xifa's lake its glaffy level fhows;

Li-po's fair ifland lay—delightful fcene!—

With fwelling flopes, and groves of every green:

On azure rocks his rich pavilion plac'd,

Rear'd its light front with golden columns

  grac'd;

High o'er the roof a weeping willow hung,

And jafmine boughs the lattice twin'd among;

In porcelain vafes crefted amaranth grew,

And ftarry after, crimfon, white, and blue;

Lien-hoa flowers upon the water fpread;

Bright fhells and corals varied luftre fhed;

       From

From fparry grottos chryftal drops diftill'd

On founding brafs, and air with mufic fill'd;

Soft thro' the bending canes the breezes play'd,

The ruftling leaves continual murmur made;

Gay fhoals of gold-fifh glitter'd in the tide,

And gaudy birds flew fportive by its fide.

The diftant profpects well the fight might pleafe,

With pointed mountains, and romantic trees:

From craggy cliffs, between the verdant fhades,

The filver rills rufh'd down in bright cafcades;

O'er terrac'd fteeps rich cotton harvefts* wav'd,

And fmooth canals the rice-clad valley lav'd;

Long rows of cyprefs† parted all the land,

And tall pagodas crown'd the river's ftrand!

---

* The Chinefe reduce the fteep flopes of their hills into little terraces, on which they grow cotton, potatoes, &c. They plant the edges of their terraces with trees, which keep up the ground, and make a very fine appearance.

† Their rice-grounds are feparated by broad ditches, the fides of which are planted with cyprefles.

Vide Ofbeck's Voyage to China.

'Twas

'Twas here, from bufinefs and its pomp and pain,

The penfive mafter fought relief in vain.

LI-PO, mild prince, a viceroy's fceptre fway'd,

And ten fair towns his gentle rule obey'd :

The morn's tranfactions to his memory came,

And fome he found to praife, and fome to blame;

Mark'd here how juftice, pity there prevail'd,

And how from hafte or indolence he fail'd.

Beneath a bower of fweet Ka-fa, whofe bloom

Fill'd all the adjacent lawn with rich perfume,

His flaves at diftance fat—a beauteous train !—

One wak'd the lute, and one the vocal ftrain :

They faw his brow with care all clouded o'er,

And wifh'd to eafe the anxiety he bore.

Amufive tales their foothing lay difclos'd,

Of heroes brave to perils ftrange expos'd;

Of tyrants proud, from power's high fummit caft;

And lovers, long defponding, bleft at laft.

They

They ceas'd; the warblings softly died away,

Like zephyrs ceasing at the close of day.

‘ This scene,' said he, ‘ how fair! to please the

 ‘ sight

‘ How Nature's charms, Art's ornaments unite!

‘ Those maids, what magic in the strains they sung!

‘ Song sweetliest flows from Beauty's tuneful tongue.

‘ Yet say, did TIEN bid power and wealth be mine,

‘ For me my soul to pleasure to resign?

 ‘ What boots that annual, on our fathers' tombs,

‘ We strew fair flowers, and offer choice perfumes;

‘ Our veneration of their memories shew,

‘ And not their steps in Virtue's path pursue?

‘ When, from his province as the prince returns,

‘ Rich feasts for him are spread, and incense burns,

‘ And gilded barks unfold their streamers gay,

‘ And following crowds their loud applauses pay;

‘ Avails all this, if he from right has swerv'd,

‘ And Conscience tells him all is undeserv'd?

       ‘ Arise,

' Arife, LI-PO ! 'tis Duty calls, arife !

' The fun finks reddening in Tartarian fkies.

' Yon walls that tower o'er Xenfi's neighbouring

  ' plain,

' Yon walls unnumber'd miferies contain.

' Think, why did TIEN fuperior rank impart,

' Force of the mind, or feelings of the heart.

' Laft night in fleep, to Fancy's fight difplay'd,

' Lay lovelier fcenes than e'er my eyes furvey'd;

' With purple fhone the hills, with gold the vales,

' And greeneft foliage wav'd in gentleft gales:

' 'Midft palmy fields, with funfhine ever bright,

' A palace rear'd its walls of filvery white;

' The gates of pearl a fhady hall difclos'd,

' Where old CONFUCIUS' rev'rend form repos'd :

' Loofe o'er his limbs the filk's light texture flow'd,

' His eye ferene etherial luftre fhow'd :

" My fon," faid he, as near his feat I drew,

" Caft round this wonderous fpot thy dazzled view;

      " See

" See how, by lucid founts in myrtle bowers,

" The bleſt inhabitants conſume their hours!

" They ne'er to War, fell Fiend! commiſſion gave

" To murder, ravage, baniſh, and enſlave;

" They ne'er bid Grandeur raiſe her gorgeous pile,

" With tribute raviſh'd from the hand of Toil;

" But parents, guardians of the people reign'd,

" The weak defended, and the poor ſuſtain'd."

' Smiling he ceas'd—the viſion ſeem'd to fly,

' Like fleecy clouds diſperſing in the ſky.

  ' Ariſe, LI-PO! and caſt thy robes aſide,

' Diſguiſe thy form, thy well-known features hide;

' Go forth, yon ſtreets, yon crowded ſtreets pervade,

' Mix with the throng, and mark who ſeeks thy

    ' aid:

' There Avarice ſtern, o'er Poverty bears ſway,

' And Age and Sickneſs fall his eaſy prey;

' There hands that Juſtice' ſacred enſigns bear,

' Protect the plunderer, and the plunder ſhare;

                              ' Perhaps

‘ Perhaps there Difcord's defperate rage prevails, }

‘ And Wifdom's voice to calm the tumult fails;

‘ Perhaps Revenge gives victims to the grave,

‘ Perhaps they perifh, ere I hafte to fave!'

He fpoke, and rofe; but now along the way

That from the city-gate fair-winding lay,

Stretch'd thro' green meads where lowing cattle graz'd,

Amid the lake's wide filver level rais'd,

Led up fteep rocks by painted bridges join'd,

Or near thin trees that o'er the tide inclin'd,

Slow tow'rds his palace came a fuppliant train;—

Whoe'er his prefence fought ne'er fought in vain—

The ready veffel, waiting at his call,

Receiv'd, and bore him to the audience-hall.

O D E S.

THE Horatian, or leſſer Ode, is characteriſed princi-
pally by eaſe and correctneſs. The following little Pieces,
attempted on that plan, were the production of very dif-
ferent periods, and, on reviſal, were thought not unde-
ſerving a place in this Collection.

O D E I.

TO LEISURE.

GENTLE Leiſure, whom of yore
    To Wealth the fair Contentment bore,
When Peace with them her dwelling made,
And Health her kind attendance paid;
As wandering o'er the ſunny plains
They fed their herds and fleecy trains:——
O Thou! who country ſcenes and air
Preferr'ſt to courts and crowds and care;
With Thee I've often paſs'd the day,
To Thee I wake the grateful lay.

With Thee on Chadwell's thymy brow*,
Beneath the hazel's bending bough,

* Chadwell: The New River Head, near Ware.

I've

I've fat to breathe the fragrance cool
Exhaling from the glaffy pool;
Where, thro' th' unfullied chryftal feen,
The bottom fhow'd its fhining green:
As, all-attentive, thefe I view'd,
And many a pleafing thought purfued,
Whate'er of pleafure they beftow'd,
Still I to Thee that pleafure ow'd!

With Thee, on Mufsla's * corn-clad height
The landfcape oft has charm'd my fight;
Delightful hills, and vales and woods,
And dufty roads, and winding floods
And towns, that thro' thin groups of h de
Their roofs of varied form difplay'd:
As, all-attentive, thefe I view'd,
And many a pleafing thought purfued,
Whate'er of pleafure they beftow'd,
Still I to Thee that pleafure ow'd!

* Mufsla: a hill on the north fide of Ware.

With

With Thee, where Eafna's* hornbeam-grove

Its foliage o'er me interwove,

Along the lonely path I've ftray'd,

By banks in hoary mofs array'd;

Where tufts of azure orpine grew,

And branchy fern of brighter hue:

As, all-attentive, thefe I view'd,

And many a pleafing thought purfued,

Whate'er of pleafure they beftow'd,

Still I to Thee that pleafure ow'd!

With Thee, by Stanfted's† farms inclos'd,

With aged elms in rows difpos'd;

Or where her chapel's walls appear,

The filver winding river near,

Beneath the broad-leav'd fycamore,

I've linger'd on the fhady fhore:

* Eafna: a pleafant wood, eaft of Ware.

† Stanfted: a village in the fame neighbourhood.

As

As, all-attentive, thefe I view'd,

And many a pleafing thought purfued,

Whate'er of pleafure they beftow'd,

Still I to Thee that pleafure ow'd !

With Thee, where Thames his waters leads

Round Poplar's Ifle* of verdant meads,

Along the undulating tide,

I've feen the white-fail'd veffels glide ;

Or gaz'd on London's lofty towers,

Or Dulwich hills, or Greenwich bowers :

As, all-attentive, thefe I view'd,

And many a pleafing thought purfued,

Whate'er of pleafure they beftow'd,

Still I to Thee that pleafure ow'd !

O gentle Leifure !—abfent long—

I woo thee with this tuneful fong :

* Poplar's Ifle ; commonly called The Ifle of Dogs, oppofite Greenwich.

If

If e'er, allur'd by grateful change,

O'er fcenes yet unbeheld I range,

And Albion's eaft or weftern fhore

For rural folitudes explore :

As, all-attentive, thefe I view,

And many a pleafing thought purfue,

Whate'er of pleafure they beftow,

To Thee that pleafure I muft owe!

O D E II.

THE EVENING WALK.

———————————

WHAT time fair Spring, with dewy hand,
    Awakes her cowſlip bloom;
And hawthorn boughs, by breezes fann'd,
    Diffuſe a rich perfume:

Young THERON down the valley ſtray'd
    At evening's ſilent hour;
When bright the ſetting ſunbeams play'd
    On Hertford's diſtant tower.

He ſigh'd, and caſt around his eye
    O'er all the pleaſing ſcene;
Now tow'rds the golden-clouded ſky,
    Now on the fields of green.

4   ' Thrice

‘ Thrice has fair Spring her cowslip bloom

 ‘ Awak’d with dewy hand;

‘ And hawthorn boughs diffus’d perfume,

 ‘ By western breezes fann’d;

‘ Since here, at evening’s silent hour,

 ‘ Delighted oft I stray’d;

‘ While bright on Hertford’s distant tower

 ‘ The setting sunbeams play’d:

‘ ’Twas then the flatterer Hope was near,

 ‘ And sung this soothing strain:

“ Where thro’ the trees yon tow’rs appear

 “ Far o’er the level plain;

“ There oft thy pleasant evening walk

 “ Thy favourite Maid shall join,

“ And all the charms of tender talk

 “ And tuneful song be thine:

       “ With

" With thee she'll hear the bleat of flocks,

 " The throstle's mellow lay ;

" The rills that murmur o'er the rocks,

 " The whispers of the spray."—

' So sung false Hope—Deceiv'd I heard,

 ' And set my heart at ease ;

' The future then so fair appear'd,

 ' It made the present please.

' So sung false Hope—The approaching years,

 ' That distant look'd so gay,

' With clouds of cares and storms of fears

 ' All fraught, have pass'd away.

' As glides yon sun adown the sky,

 ' As rolls yon rapid stream ;

' So fast our joys and sorrows fly,

 ' And flown appear a dream.

       ' Be

' Be then the events that Time has brought,

  ' To me not brought in vain ;

' By painful difappointment taught,

  ' Let wifdom be my gain !'

Thus THERON fpoke, and earneft eyed

  The fun's departing ray ;

Again he look'd, again he figh'd,

  And homeward bent his way.

O D E III.

TO CHILDHOOD.

———————

CHILDHOOD! happieſt ſtage of life,
    Free from care and free from ſtrife,
Free from Memory's ruthleſs reign,
Fraught with ſcenes of former pain;
Free from Fancy's cruel ſkill,
Fabricating future ill;
Time, when all that meets the view,
All can charm, for all is new;
How thy long-loſt hours I mourn,
Never, never, to return!

    Then to toſs the circling ball,
Caught rebounding from the wall;

Then

Then the mimic ſhip to guide

Down the kennel's dirty tide;

Then the hoop's revolving pace

Thro' the duſty ſtreet to chace;

O what joy!—it once was mine,

Childhood, matchleſs boon of thine!—

How thy long-loſt hours I mourn,

Never, never, to return!

O D E IV.

HEARING MUSIC.

———————

YON organ! hark!—how foft, how fweet,
 The warbling notes in concert meet!
  The found my fancy leads
To climes where Phœbus' brighteft beams
Gild jafmine groves and chryftal ftreams
  And lily-mantled meads;

Where myrtle bowers their bloom unfolc
Where citrons bend with fruit of gold,
  Where grapes deprefs the vines;
Where, on the bank with rofes gay,
Love, Innocence, and Pleafure play,
  And Beauty's form reclines.

Now

Now different tones and meaſures flow,

And, gravely deep, and ſadly flow,

   Involve the mind in gloom;

I ſeem to join the mournful train,

Attendant round the couch of Pain,

   Or leaning o'er the tomb:

To where the orphan'd infant ſleeps,

To where the love-lorn damſel weeps,

   I pitying ſeem to ſtray;

Methinks I watch his cradle near;

Methinks her drooping thoughts I chear,

   And wipe her tears away.

Now loud the tuneful thunders roll,

And rouſe and elevate the ſoul

   O'er earth and all its care;

I ſeem to hear from heavenly plains

Angelic choirs reſponſive ſtrains,

   And in their raptures ſhare.

N

O D E V.

A L A N D S C A P E.

ON the eaſtern hill's ſteep ſide
 Spreads the rural hamlet wide;
'Croſs the vale, where willows riſe,
Further ſtill another lies;
And, beneath a ſteeper hill,
Lies another further ſtill:
Near them many a field and grove—
Scenes where Health and Labour rove!

 Northward ſwelling ſlopes are ſeen,
Clad with corn-fields neat and green;
There, thro' graſſy plains below,
Broad and ſmooth the waters flow;
While the town, their banks along,
Bids its cluſtering houſes throng,

In

In the funfhine glittering fair;
Haunts of Bufinefs, haunts of Care!

Weftward o'er the yellow meads
Wind the rills thro' waving reeds;
From dark elms a fhadow falls
On the abbey's whiten'd walls:
Wide the park's green lawns expand;
Thick its tufted lindens ftand:
Fair retreat! that well might pleafe
Wealth, and Elegance, and Eafe.

Hark! amidft the diftant fhades
Murmuring drop the deep cafcades;
Hark! amidft the ruftling trees
Softly fighs the gentle breeze:
And the Eolian harp, reclin'd
Obvious to the ftream of wind,
Pours its wildly-warbled ftrain,
Rifing now, now funk again.

How

How the view detains the fight!

How the founds the ear delight !—

Sweet the fcene! but think not there

Happinefs fincere to fhare :

Reafon ftill regrets the day

Paffing rapidly away ;

Leffening Life's too little ftore ;

Paffing, to return no more !

O D E VI.

TO A FRIEND,

ON HIS MARRIAGE, AND REMOVAL INTO THE COUNTRY.

[Written at Stanway-Hall, in Effex.]

WHATE'ER of lighter ftrain the Mufe

Effay'd, in vacant hours of eafe,

At thy expence to raife a fmile,

I deem thy candour will excufe;

For fure I meant not to difpleafe,

For fure I wifh'd thee well the while *.

---

* The Author alludes to fome trifling pieces of humour, written on his Friend, for the amufement of a few intimate acquaintance.

And

And now the nuptial knot is tied,

That Mufe no idle flattery brings,

Nor talks of joy unmixt with care—

I truft that none who e'er has tried

The fober ftate of human things,

Will give thee hope fuch joy to fhare.

Domeftic Life muft foon be thine—

'Tis various as an April day;

'Tis pleafure now, and now 'tis pain:

Thro' ftorms of foul and gleams of fine

Contented hold thy fteady way,

And thefe enjoy, and thofe fuftain.

From London's ftreets to folitude,

From brilliant fhops to dirty fields,

From beaux and belles to rugged hinds—

The change I own is ftrange and rude:

Yet fcarce a place fo little yields,

But he who feeks amufement finds.

Perchance

Perchance thou'lt not difdain to hear

The ploughman's hiftory of the plain;

'Thy fight the profpect's fcenes may charm;

And fure faftidious is the ear,

That flights the milkmaid's fimple ftrain,

At evening echoing from the farm.

The market lore of artful fwains;

The price of cattle and of corn,

The fportfman's feats of dogs and guns;—

To practife that will coft thee pains;

And thefe with patience muft be born,

For he will be diflik'd who fhuns.

Courage, my friend! whate'er our fate;

So verfatile the human mind,

That oft, when novelty is o'er,

To objects of our former hate

Affimilated and refign'd,

We wonder they difpleas'd before.

'Twas

'Twas on the festive, social day,

Where Beauty cast her smiles around,

And Mirth the mind from care reliev'd;

What time our hands in harmless play

Thy brow with wreaths of myrtle bound,

My thoughts this grateful lay conceiv'd.

From Stanway's groves, from fields of Layer*,

To other scenes and other friends

To-morrow calls my steps away;

Yet Memory them in view shall bear;

Yet them the wish of health attends,

And many a moment calm and gay.

* Layer Breton : a village in Essex.

O D E VII.

WRITTEN IN WINTER.

———————

WHILE in the sky black clouds impend,
    And fogs arise, and rains descend,
And one brown prospect opens round
Of leafless trees and furrow'd ground;
Save where unmelted spots of snow
Upon the shaded hill-side show;
    While chill winds blow, and torrents roll,
The scene disgusts the sight, depresses all the soul.

    Yet worse what polar climates share—
Vast regions, dreary, bleak, and bare!—
There, on an icy mountain's height,
Seen only by the moon's pale light,

4

Stern

Stern Winter rears his giant form,

His robe a mift, his voice a ftorm :

His frown the fhivering nations fly,

And hid for half the year in fmoky caverns lie,

Yet there the lamp's perpetual blaze

Can pierce the gloom with chearing rays;

Yet there the heroic tale or fong

Can urge the lingering hours along;

Yet there their hands with timely care

The kajak * and the dart prepare,

On fummer feas to work their way,

And wage the watry war, and make the feals their prey.

Too Delicate ! reproach no more

The feafons of thy native fhore—

There foon fhall Spring defcend the fky,

With fmiling brow and placid eye ;

* Kajak : a Greenland fifhing-boat.

A prim-

A primrofe wreath furrounds her hair,

Her green robe floats upon the air;

And, fcatter'd from her liberal hand,

Fair bloffoms deck the trees, fair flow'rs adorn the

land.

O D E VIII.

TO A FRIEND.

———————

WHERE Grove-hill* ſhows thy villa fair,
But late, my LETTSOM, there with thee
'Twas mine the tranquil hour to ſhare—
The ſocial hour of converſe free ;
To mark the arrangement of thy ground,
And all the pleaſing proſpect round,
Where, while we gaz'd, new beauties ſtill were
found.

There, as the impending cloud of ſmoke
Fled various from the varying gale,
Full on the view freſh objects broke
Along the extenſive peopled vale,

* At Camberwell, in Surry.

Beſide

Beside Thamesis' bending stream,

From ancient Lambeth's west extreme,

To   Limehouse   glittering   in   the   evening

  beam.

And now and then the glancing eye

Caught glimpse of spots remoter still,

On Hampstead's street-clad slope so high,

Or Harrow's far conspicuous hill;

Or eastward wander'd to explore

All Peckham's pleasant level o'er,

To busy Deptford's vessel-crowded shore:

Or sought that southern landscape's bound,

Those swelling mounts—one smooth and green,

And one with oaken coverts crown'd,

And one where scattering trees are seen *.

   * The Dulwich hills.

         'Twas

'Twas thefe, with Summer's radiance bright,

That gave my earlieft youth delight,

Of rural fcenes the firft that met my fight *.

That Bufinefs, with fatiguing cares,

For this delightful feat of thine

Such fcanty ftore of moments fpares,

Say, Friend, fhall I for thee repine?—

Were it the commerce of the main,

Or culture of the teeming plain,

From blame or pity I fhould fcarce refrain.

But O! to alleviate human woes,

To banifh ficknefs, banifh pain,

To give the fleeplefs eye repofe,

The nervelefs arm its ftrength again;

From parent eyes to dry the tear,

The wife's diftrefsful thought to chear,

And end the hufband's and the lover's fear;

* The Author was born in the environs of London, on the Surry fide.

Where

Where Want fits pining, faint, and ill,

To lend thy kind, unpurchas'd aid,

And hear the exertions of thy fkill

With many a grateful blefling paid—

'Tis luxury to the feeling heart,

Beyond what focial hours impart,

Or Nature's beauteous fcenes, or curious works

  of Art!

O D E   IX.

LEAVING BATH, MDCCLXXVI.

———————

BATH ! ere I quit thy pleafing fcene,
   Thy Beachen cliff I'll climb again,
To view thy mountains vivid green,
To view thy hill-furrounded plain :
   To fee diftinct beneath the eye,
   As in a pictur'd profpect nigh,
Thofe Attic ftructures fhining white,
That form thy funny crefcent's bend,
Or by thy dufty ftreets extend,
Or near thy winding river's fite.

Did Commerce thefe proud piles upraife ?
For thee fhe ne'er unfurl'd her fails—
HYGEIA gave thy fountains praife,
And Pain and Languor fought thy vales:

But

But thefe fuffic'd an humble cell,

   If they with Strength and Eafe might dwell.

Then Fafhion call'd; his potent voice

Proud Wealth with ready ftep obey'd,

And Pleafure all her arts effay'd,

To fix with thee the fickle choice.

Precarious gift!—Thy manfions gay,

Where Peers and Beauties lead the ball,

Neglected, foon may feel decay;

Forfaken, moulder to their fall.—

   Palmyra, once like thee renown'd,

   Now lies a ruin on the ground.—

But ftill thy environs fo fair,

Thy waters falutary aid,

Will furely always fome perfuade

To render thee their care.

O

O D E   X.

O FRIEND! to Thee, whofe liberal mind
   Was form'd with tafte for joys refin'd,
For all the extended country yields,
Of azure fkies and verdant fields;
For all that Genius' hand difplays,—
The Painter's forms, the Poet's lays:—
To Thee, reftraint to that dull room,
Where funfhine never breaks the gloom;
To Thee, reftraint to that dull lore
Of books, with numbers cypher'd o'er—
How hard the lot! I fee with pain,
And wifh it oft exchang'd in vain.

   Yet not for Thee I afk the ftores
Which Rapine rends from foreign fhores,

Nor

Nor thofe Oppreffion's power procures

From ills that Poverty endures.

Far happier Thou! thy honeft gain

Can life with decency fuftain;

For Thee, Content, with thought ferene,

Surveys the prefent changeful fcene;

And Piety her view fublime

Extends beyond the realm of Time.

O D E XI.

TO A FRIEND APPREHENSIVE OF DECLINING
FRIENDSHIP.

———

TOO much in Man's imperfect ftate
 Miftake produces ufelefs pain.—
Methinks, of Friendfhip's frequent fate
 I hear my FROGLEY's voice complain.

This heart, I hope, forgives its foes;
 I know it ne'er forgets its friends;
Where'er may Chance my fteps difpofe,
 The abfent oft my thought attends.

Deem not that Time's oblivious hand
 From Memory's page has ras'd the days,
By Lee's green verge we wont to ftand,
 And on his chryftal current gaze.

From

From Chadwell's cliffs, o'erhung with fhade,
From Widbury's profpect-yielding hill,
Sweet look'd the fcenes we then furvey'd,
While Fancy fought for fweeter ftill:

Then how did Learning's ftores delight!
From books what pleafures then we drew!
For then their charms firft met our fight,
And then their faults we little knew.

Alas! Life's Summer fwiftly flies,
And few its hours of bright and fair!
Why bid Diftruft's chill eaft-wind rife,
To blaft the fcanty blooms they bear?

O D E XII.

TO A FRIEND.

———————

NO, COCKFIELD, no! I'll not difdain
    Thy Upton's elm-divided plain;
Nor fcorn the varied views it yields,
O'er Bromley's creeks and ifles of reeds,
Or Ham's or Plaiftow's level meads,
To Woolwich ftreets, or Charlton fields:
Thy hedge-row paths I'll pleafant call,
And praife the lonely lane that leads
To that old tower upon the wall.

  'Twas when Misfortune's ftroke fevere,
And Melancholy's prefence drear,

Had

Had made my Amwell's groves difpleafe,

That thine my weary fteps receiv'd,

And much the change my mind reliev'd,

And much thy kindnefs gave me eafe ;

For o'er the paft as thought would ftray,

That thought thy voice as oft retriev'd,

To fcenes which fair before us lay.

And there, in happier hours, the walk

Has frequent pleas'd with friendly talk ;

From theme to theme that wander'd ftill—

The long detail of where we had been,

And what we had heard, and what we had feen ;

And what the Poet's tuneful fkill,

And what the Painter's graphic art,

Or Antiquarian's fearches keen,

Of calm amufement could impart.

Then oft did Nature's works engage,

And oft we fearch'd LINNÆUS' page ;

The Scanian Sage, whofe wond'rous toil

Had clafs'd the vegetable race :

And curious, oft from place to place,

We rang'd, and fought each different foil,

Each different plant intent to view,

And all the marks minute to trace,

Whence he his nice diftinctions drew.

O moments thefe, not ill employ'd !

O moments, better far enjoy'd

Than thofe in crowded cities pafs'd ;

Where oft to Luxury's gaudy reign

Trade lends her feeble aid in vain,

Till Pride, a bankrupt wretch at laft,

Bids Fraud his fpecious wiles effay,

Youth's eafy confidence to gain,

Or Induftry's poor pittance rend away !

O D E XIII.

I HATE that drum's difcordant found,
 Parading round, and round, and round:
To thoughtlefs youth it pleafure yields,
And lures from cities and from fields,
To fell their liberty for charms
Of tawdry lace, and glittering arms;
And when Ambition's voice commands,
To march, and fight, and fall, in foreign lands.

 I hate that drum's difcordant found,
Parading round, and round, and round:
To me it talks of ravag'd plains,
And burning towns, and ruin'd fwains,
And mangled limbs, and dying groans,
And widows tears, and orphans moans;
And all that Mifery's hand beftows,
To fill the catalogue of human woes.

7

O D E XIV.

WRITTEN AFTER READING SOME MODERN
LOVE-VERSES.

———————

TAKE hence this tuneful Trifler's lays!
   I'll hear no more the unmeaning ſtrain
Of Venus' doves, and Cupid's darts,
And killing eyes, and wounded hearts;
All Flattery's round of fulſome praiſe,
All Falſehood's cant of fabled pain.

   Bring me the Muſe whoſe tongue has told
Love's genuine plaintive tender tale;
Bring me the Muſe whoſe ſounds of woe
'Midſt Death's dread ſcenes ſo ſweetly flow,
When Friendſhip's faithful breaſt lies cold,
When Beauty's blooming cheek is pale:

Bring

Bring thefe—I like their grief fincere;

It fooths my fympathetic gloom:

For, oh! Love's genuine pains I've borne,

And Death's dread rage has made me mourn;

I've wept o'er Friendfhip's early bier,

And dropt the tear on Beauty's tomb.

O D E XV.

THE MUSE; OR, POETICAL ENTHUSIASM.

***

THE Muſe! whate'er the Muſe inſpires,

My ſoul the tuneful ſtrain admires:

The Poet's birth, I aſk not where,

His place, his name, they're not my care;

Nor Greece nor Rome delights me more

Than Tagus' bank*, or Thames's ſhore †:

From ſilver Avon's flowery ſide

Tho' SHAKESPEARE's numbers ſweetly glide,

As ſweet, from Morven's deſart hills,

My ear the voice of OSSIAN fills.

***

* *Tagus' bank:* alluding to Camoens, the epic poet of Portugal; of whoſe Luſiad we have a well known maſterly tranſlation by Mr. Mickle.

† *Thames's ſhore:* alluding to Milton, Pope, &c.

The Mufe! whate'er the Mufe infpires,

My foul the tuneful ftrain admires :

Nor bigot zeal, nor party rage

Prevail, to make me blame the page ;

I fcorn not all that DRYDEN fings

Becaufe he flatters courts and kings ;

And from the mafter lyre of GRAY

When pomp of mufic breaks away,

Not lefs the found my notice draws,

For that 'tis heard in Freedom's caufe.

The Mufe! whate'er the Mufe infpires,

My foul the tuneful ftrain admires :

Where Wealth's bright fun propitious fhines,

No added luftre marks the lines ;

Where Want extends her chilling fhades,

No pleafing flower of Fancy fades ;

A fcribbling peer's applauded lays

Might claim, but claim in vain, my praife

From

From that poor Youth, whofe tales relate

Sad Juga's fears and Bawdin's fate *.

The Mufe! whate'er the Mufe infpires,

My foul the tuneful ftrain admires :

When Fame her wreath well-earn'd beftows,

My breaft no latent envy knows ;

My Langhorne's verfe I lov'd to hear,

And Beattie's fong delights my ear ;

And his, whom Athens' Tragic Maid

Now leads through Scarning's lonely glade,

While he for Britifh nymphs bids flow

Her notes of terror and of woe †.

The Mufe! whate'er the Mufe infpires,

My foul the tuneful ftrain admires :

* See Rowley's Poems, fuppofed to have been written by Chatterton, an unhappy youth born at Briftol.

† See Mr. Potter's excellent Tranflation of Æfchylus and Euripides.

Or

Or be the verfe or blank or rhyme,

The theme or humble or fublime;

If Paftoral's hand my journey leads

Thro' harveft fields or new-mown meads;

If Epic's voice fonorous calls

To Œta's cliffs * or Salem's walls † ;

Enough—the Mufe, the Mufe infpires!

My foul the tuneful ftrain admires.

---

* See Mr. Glover's Leonidas, alluded to as an example of Claffical dignity and fimplicity.

† See Taffo's Jerufalem Delivered, alluded to as an example of Gothic fancy and magnificence.

O D E   XVI.

———————

HOW fteep yon mountains rife around,
    How bold yon gloomy woods afcend!
How loud the rufhing torrents found
That 'midft thefe heaps of ruin bend,
Where one arch'd gateway yet remains,
And one lone aifle its roof retains,
And one tall turret's walls impend!

    Here once a felf-fequefter'd train
Renounc'd life's tempting pomp and glare;
Rejected power, relinquifh'd gain,
And fhunn'd the great, and fhunn'd the fair:

The

The voluntary flaves of toil,

By day they till'd their little foil,

By night they awoke, and rofe to prayer.

 Tho' Superftition much we blame,

That bade them thus confume their years;

Their motive ftill our praife muft claim,

Their conftancy our thought reveres:

And fure their folitary fcheme

Muft check each paffion's wild extreme,

And fave them cares, and fave them fears.

 Their convent's round contain'd their all;

Their minds no fad prefage oppreft,

What fate might abfent wealth befal,

How abfent friends might be diftreft:

Domeftic ills ne'er hurt their eafe;

They nought of pain could feel from thefe,

Who no domeftic joys poffeft.

P   But

But Imperfection haunts each place:

Would this kind calm atone to thee

For Fame's or Fortune's fprightly chace,

Whofe prize in profpect ftill we fee;

Or Hymen's happy moments bleft,

With Beauty leaning on thy breaft,

Or Childhood prattling at thy knee?

O D E XVII.

P R I V A T E E R I N G,

———————

HOW Cuſtom ſteels the human breaſt
    To deeds that Nature's thoughts deteſt!
How Cuſtom conſecrates to fame
What Reaſon elſe would give to ſhame!
Fair Spring ſupplies the favouring gale,
The Naval Plunderer ſpreads his ſail,
And ploughing wide the watry way,
Explores with anxious eyes his prey.

  The man he never ſaw before,
The man who him no quarrel bore,
He meets, and Avarice prompts the fight;
And Rage enjoys the dreadful ſight

Of

Of decks with ſtreaming crimſon dy'd,

And wretches ſtruggling in the tide,

Or, 'midſt th' exploſion's horrid glare,

Diſpers'd with quivering limbs in air.

The merchant now on foreign ſhores

His captur'd wealth in vain deplores;

Quits his fair home, O mournful change!

For the dark priſon's ſcanty range;

By Plenty's hand ſo lately fed,

Depends on caſual alms for bread;

And, with a father's anguiſh torn,

Sees his poor offspring left forlorn.

And yet, ſuch Man's misjudging mind,

For all this injury to his kind,

The proſperous Robber's native plain

Shall bid him welcome home again;

His name the ſong of every ſtreet,

His acts the theme of all we meet,

And

And oft the artiſt's ſkill ſhall place
To public view his pictur'd face !

  If glory thus be earn'd, for me
My object glory ne'er ſhall be ;
No, firſt in Cambria's lonelieſt dale
Be mine to hear the ſhepherd's tale !
No, firſt on Scotia's bleakeſt hill
Be mine the ſtubborn ſoil to till !
Remote from wealth, to dwell alone,
And die, to guilty praiſe unknown !

O D E XVIII.

TO HOSPITALITY.

———————

DOMESTIC Power! erewhile rever'd
 Where Syria fpread her palmy plain,
Where Greece her tuneful Mufes heard,
 Where Rome beheld her Patriot Train;
  Thou to Albion too wert known,
  'Midft the moat and mofs-grown wall
 That girt her Gothic-ftructur'd hall
  With rural trophies ftrown.

The traveller, doubtful of his way,
 Upon the pathlefs foreft wild;
The huntfman, in the heat of day,
 And with the tedious chace o'ertoil'd;

        Wide

Wide their view around them caft,

Mark'd the diftant ruftic tower,

And fought and found the feftive bower,

And fhar'd the free repaft.

E'en now, on Caledonia's fhore,

When Eve's dun robe the fky arrays,

Thy punctual hand unfolds the door,

Thy eye the mountain road furveys;

Pleas'd to fpy the cafual gueft,

Pleas'd with food his heart to cheer,

With pipe or fong to footh his ear,

And fpread his couch for reft.

Nor yet ev'n here difdain'd thy fway,

Where Grandeur's fplendid modern feat

Far o'er the landfcape glitters gay;

Or where fair Quiet's lone retreat

P 4 Hides

Hides beneath the hoary hill,

Near the dufky upland fhade,

Between the willow's glofly glade,

And by the tinkling rill.

There thine the pleafing interviews

That friends and relatives endear,

When fcenes not often feen amufe,

When tales not often told we hear;

There the fcholar's liberal mind

Oft inftruction gives and gains,

And oft the lover's lore obtains

His fair-one's audience kind.

O gentle Power! where'er thy reign,

May Health and Peace attend thee ftill;

Nor Folly's prefence caufe thee pain,

Nor Vice reward thy good with ill:

Gratitude

Gratitude thy altar raife,

Wealth to thee her offerings pay,

And Genius wake his tuneful lay

To celebrate thy praife.

O D E XIX.

THE APOLOGY.

———————

‘ PASTORAL, and Elegy, and Ode!
　　‘ Who hopes, by thefe, applaufe to gain,
‘ Believe me, Friend, may hope in vain——
‘ Thefe claffic things are not the mode;
‘ Our tafte polite, fo much refin’d,
‘ Demands a ftrain of different kind.

　‘ Go, court the Mufe of Chevy Chace,
‘ To tell in STERNHOLD’s fimple rhymes
‘ Some tale of ancient Englifh times;
‘ Or try to win rude Satire’s grace,
‘ That Scold, who dirt around her throws,
‘ And many a random ftain beftows.

　　　　　　　　　　　　　　‘ Or

' Or dull trite thoughts in fongs combine,

' And bid the tuneful accents fall,

' To wake the echoes of Vauxhall;

' Or tow'rds the Stage thy thoughts incline,

' And furnifh fome half-pilfer'd play,

' To fhine the meteor of the day.'

O! no—tho' fuch the crowd amufe,

And peals of noify praife procure;

Will they the critic eye endure,

And pafs the ordeal of Reviews?

And who is he for whom they'll gain

A nich in Fame's immortal fane?

The plan that VIRGIL's choice could claim,

The plan that HORACE deign'd to chufe,

Truft me, I wifh not to refufe:—

To AKENSIDE's or SHENSTONE's name

The praife that future days fhall pay,

Methinks may well content my lay.

5

O D E   XX.

―――――――

THIS scene how rich from Thames's side,
　　While evening suns their amber beam
Spread o'er the glaffy-surfac'd tide,
And 'midft the mafts and cordage gleam;
Blaze on the roofs with turrets crown'd,
And gild green paftures ftretch'd around,
And gild the flope of that high ground,
Whofe cornfields bright the profpect bound*!

　The white fails glide along the fhore,
　Red ftreamers on the breezes play,
　The boatmen ply the dafhing oar,
　And wide their various freight convey;

* Shooter's Hill.　This view was taken on the North fide of
the Thames, at Ratcliff.

Some

Some Neptune's hardy thoughtlefs train,

And fome the careful fons of gain, ·

And fome the enamour'd nymph and fwain

Liftening to mufic's foothing ftrain,

But there, while thefe the fight allure,

Still Fancy wings her flight away,

To woods reclufe, and vales obfcure,

And ftreams that folitary ftray;

To view the pine-grove on the hill,

The rocks that trickling fprings diftill,

The meads that quivering afpins fill,

Or alders crowding o'er the rill.

And where the trees unfold their bloom,

And where the banks their floriage bear,

And all effufe a rich perfume

That hovers in the foft calm air;

The hedge-row path to wind along,

To hear the bleating fleecy throng,

To

To hear the fkylark's airy fong,

And throftle's note fo clear and ftrong.

   But fay, if there our fteps were brought,

Would thefe their pow'r to pleafe retain?

Say, would not reftlefs, roving thought

Turn back to bufy fcenes again?

O ftrange formation of the mind!

Still, tho' the prefent fair we find,

Still tow'rds the abfent thus inclin'd,

Thus fix'd on objects left behind!

O D E   XXI.

———————

THEE, BRISTOL, oft my thoughts recal,
　　Thy Kingſdown brow and Brandon hill ;
The ſpace, once circled by thy wall,
　　Which tow'rs and ſpires of churches fill ;
And maſts and ſails of veſſels tall,
With trees and houſes intermingled ſtill ! !

From Clifton's rocks how grand the ſight,
　　When Avon's dark tide ruſh'd between !
How grand, from Henbury's woody height,
　　The Severn's wide-ſpread watry ſcene,
Her waves with trembling ſunſhine bright,
And Cambrian hills beyond them riſing green !

　　　　　　　　　　　　　　To

To Mendip's ridge how ſtretch'd away

My view, while Fancy ſought the plain

Where Blagdon's groves ſecluded lay,

And heard my much-lov'd Poet's ſtrain*!

Ah! why ſo near, nor thither ſtray

To meet the friend I ne'er ſhall meet again?

Occaſion's call averſe to prize,

Irreſolute we oft remain—

She ſoon irrevocably flies,

And then we mourn her flown in vain;

While Pleaſure's imag'd forms ariſe,

Whoſe fancied loſs Regret beholds with pain.

And Bristol! why thy ſcenes explore,

And why thoſe ſcenes ſo ſoon reſign,

And fail to ſeek the ſpot that bore

That wonderous tuneful Youth of thine,

* The late ingenious Dr. John Langhorne, then reſident at Blagdon, near Briſtol.

The

The Bard *, whofe boafted ancient ftore

Rofe recent from his own exhauftlefs mine †!

Though Fortune all her gifts denied,

 Though Learning made him not her choice,

The Mufe ftill placed him at her fide,

 And bade him in her fmile rejoice—

Defcription ftill his pen fupplied,

Pathos his thought, and Melody his voice!

Confcious and proud of merit high,

 Fame's wreath he boldly claim'd to wear;

But Fame, regardlefs, pafs'd him by,

 Unknown, or deem'd unworth her care:

The Sun of Hope forfook his fky;

And all his land look'd dreary, bleak, and bare!

* Chatterton.

† This is at leaft the Author's opinion, notwithftanding all
that has hitherto appeared on the other fide of the queftion.
The laft line alludes to one of the ingenious Mr. Mafon in his
Elegy to a young Nobleman :

  " See from the depths of his exhauftlefs mine

  " His glittering ftores the tuneful fpendthrift throws."

Then Poverty, grim fpectre, rofe,

     And horror o'er the profpect threw—

His deep diftrefs too nice to expofe ;

     Too nice for common aid to fue,

A dire alternative he chofe,

And rafhly from the painful fcene withdrew.

     Ah ! why for Genius' headftrong rage

       Did Virtue's hand no curb prepare?

What boots, poor youth ! that now thy page

     Can boaft the publick praife to fhare,

The learn'd in deep refearch engage,

And lightly entertain the gentle fair ?

     Ye, who fuperfluous wealth command,

       O why your kind relief delay'd ?

O why not fnatch'd his defperate hand ?

     His foot on Fate's dread brink not ftay'd?

What thanks had you your native land

For a new SHAKESPEARE or new MILTON paid?

                         For

For me—Imagination's power

   Leads oft infenfibly my way,

To where, at midnight's filent hour,

   The crefcent moon's flow-weftering ray

Pours full on REDCLIFF's lofty tower,

And gilds with yellow light its walls of grey.

'Midft Toil and Commerce flumbering round,

   Lull'd by the rifing tide's hoarfe roar,

There Frome and Avon willow-crown'd,

   I view fad-wandering by the fhore,

With ftreaming tears, and notes of mournful found,

Too late their haplefs Bard, untimely loft, deplore.

O D E XXII.

TO CRITICISM.

FAIR Nymph! of Tafte and Learning born,
 Whom Truth's and Candour's gifts adorn,
The Mufe's friend! to thee fhe fings:
Accept the grateful verfe fhe brings.

When Genius, ranging Nature o'er,
Collects his tributary ftore,
What Matter's tract immenfe fupplies,
Or wide in Mind's vaft region lies,
And every thought with fkill combines,
And all tranfmits in tuneful lines;
Then rapture fparkling in thine eye,
Then rais'd thy folemn voice on high;
Thy comment ftill his work purfues,
The plan explains, the ftyle reviews,
And marks its ftrength, and marks its eafe;
And tells us why and how they pleafe.

       And

And when, perhaps, difdaining care,

He blends with faults his products fair;

Whate'er of fuch thy fight furveys,

Thy tongue in triumph ne'er difplays,

But hints, as fpots that dim the fun,

Or rocks that future fails fhould fhun.

'Twas Thee whom once Stagyra's grove

Oft with her Sage * allur'd to rove;

'Twas Thee to whom in Tadmor's bowers,

Her Statefman † vow'd his vacant hours;

'Twas Thee whom, Tibur's vines among,

Her Bard ‡ in carelefs meafures fung;

'Twas Thou who thence to Albion's plain

Remov'd, to teach her tuneful train,

When DRYDEN's age, by thee infpir'd,

Condemn'd the flights his youth admir'd;

And POPE, intent on higher praife,

So polifh'd all his pleafing lays:

* Ariftotle.   † Longinus.   ‡ Horace.

And now, by Thee, our favour'd coaſt

A WARTON, HURD, and BURKE can boaſt;

And Her, whoſe pen from Gallic rage

Defended SHAKESPEARE's injur'd page *.

   Give me, bright Power! with ready ear,

Another's plea for fame to hear,

And bid my willing voice allow

The bays to Merit's modeſt brow:

And when the Muſe her preſence deigns,

And prompts my own unſtudied ſtrains,

Inſtruct me them, with view ſevere,

To inſpect, and keep from error clear;

Nor ſpare, though fancy'd e'er ſo fine,

One ill-placed thought, or uſeleſs line.

---

   * The ingenious Mrs. Montague, who has ſo ably vindicated Shakeſpeare from the cavils of Voltaire.

O D E XXIII.

TO DISEASE.

DISEASE! Man's dread, relentless foe,

    Fell source of fear, and pain, and woe!

O say, on what ill-fated coast

They mourn thy tyrant reign the most?

On Java's bogs, or Gambia's sand,

Or Persia's sultry southern strand;

Or Egypt's annual-flooded plain,

Or Rome's neglected, waste domain;

Or where her walls Byzantium rears,

And mosques and turrets crescent-crown'd,

And from his high serail the sultan hears

The wide Propontis' beating waves resound *.

---

* *Byzantium :* Constantinople; subject to frequent visitations
of that dreadful fever, the plague.

I'll

I'll aſk no more—Our clime, tho' fair,

Enough thy tyrant reign muſt ſhare;

And lovers there, and friends, complain,

By Thee their friends and lovers ſlain:

And yet our Avarice and our Pride

Combine to ſpread thy miſchiefs wide;

While that the captive wretch confines,

To hunger, cold, and filth reſigns,—

And this the funeral pomp attends

To vaults, where mouldering corſes lie,—

Amid foul air thy form unſeen aſcends,

And like a vulture hovers in the ſky *.

---

* Alluding to the too frequent miſerable ſituation of priſoners of war, debtors, &c.; and the abſurd cuſtom of burying in churches; circumſtances contributing greatly to the propagation of Diſeaſe.

O D E XXIV.

THE TEMPESTUOUS EVENING.

———————

THERE's grandeur in this founding ftorm,
　　That drives the hurrying clouds along
That on each other feem to throng,
And mix in many a varied form;
While, burfting now and then between,
The Moon's dim mifty orb is feen,
And cafts faint glimpfes on the green.

Beneath the blaft the forefts bend,
And thick the branchy ruin lies,
And wide the fhower of foliage flies;
The lake's black waves in tumult blend,
Revolving o'er and o'er and o'er,
And foaming on the rocky fhore,
Whofe caverns echo to their roar.

3　　　　　　　　　　　　The

The fight fublime enrapts my thought,

And fwift along the paft it ftrays,

And much of ftrange event furveys,

What Hiftory's faithful tongue has taught,

Or Fancy form'd, whofe plaftic fkill

The page with fabled change can fill

Of ill to good, or good to ill.

But can my foul the fcene enjoy,

That rends another's breaft with pain?

O haplefs he, who, near the main,

Now fees its billowy rage deftroy!

Beholds the foundering bark defcend,

Nor knows, but what its fate may end

The moments of his deareft friend!

O D E   XXV.

THE MELANCHOLY EVENING.

———————

O HASTE, ye hovering clouds, away,
 Ye clouds fo fleecy, dim, and pale,
Thro' which the Moon's obftructed ray
 Sheds this fad whitenefs o'er the vale!
Forbear, ye bells, that languid ftrain!
The fight, the found, are fraught with pain;
The words of dying friends I hear,
The open grave I linger near,
Take the laft look, and drop the parting tear!

Before my view dire phantoms rife,
 The plagues of haplefs human-kind!
Pale Fear, who unpurfued ftill flies,
 And ftarts, and turns, and looks behind;
      Rem o rfe

Remorfe, whofe own indignant aim

Deforms with ufelefs wounds her frame;

Defpair, whofe tongue no fpeech will deign,

Whofe ghaftly brow looks dark difdain,

And bends from fteep rocks o'er the foaming main,

And Rage, whofe bofom inly burns,

While Reafon's call he fcorns to hear;

And Jealoufy, who ruthlefs turns

From fuppliant Beauty's prayer and tear;

Revenge, whofe thoughts tumultuous roll

To feek the poniard or the bowl;

And Phrenfy, wildly paffing by,

With her chain'd arm and ftarting eye,

And voice that with loud curfes rends the fky!

Ambition, here, to heights of power

His courfe with daring ftep purfues,

Tho' Danger's frown againft him lour,

Tho' Guilt his path with blood beftrews;

There

There Avarice grasps his useless store,

Tho' Misery's plaints his aid implore,

Tho' he, her ruin'd cottage nigh,

Beholds her famish'd infants lie,

And hears their faint, their last expiring cry!

Ye dreadful band! O spare, O spare!

   Alas, your ear no prayers persuade!

But, ah! if Man your reign must bear,

   Sure Man had better ne'er been made!

Say, will Religion clear this gloom,

And point to bliss beyond the tomb?

Yes, haply for her chosen train;

The rest, they say, stern decrees ordain

To realms of endless night, and everlasting pain*!

---

* The Author does not give these as his own sentiments, but merely such as the gloomy moment described might naturally suggest. That the above dreadful idea is adopted by a large body of Christians, is sufficient to authorise its admission into a Poem professing to paint the dark side of things.

O D E XXVI.

THE PLEASANT EVENING.

––––––––

DELIGHTFUL looks this clear, calm ſky,
    With CYNTHIA's ſilver orb on high;
Delightful looks this ſmooth green ground,
With ſhadows caſt from cots around :
Quick-twinkling luſtre decks the tide;
And chearful radiance gently falls
On that white town, and caſtle walls,
That crown the ſpacious river's further ſide.

    And now along the echoing hills
The night-bird's ſtrain melodious trills;
And now the echoing dale along
Soft flows the ſhepherd's tuneful ſong:
And now, wide o'er the water borne,
The city's mingled murmur ſwells,

And

And lively change of diſtant bells,
And varied warbling of the deep-ton'd horn.

Their influence calms the ſoften'd ſoul,
The paſſions feel their ſtrong controul:
While Fancy's eye, where'er it ſtrays,
A ſcene of happineſs ſurveys ;
Thro' all the various walks of life
No natural ill nor moral ſees,
No Famine fell, nor dire Diſeaſe,
Nor War's infernal unrelenting ſtrife.

For theſe, behold a heavenly band
Their white wings waving o'er the land!
Sweet Innocence, a cherub fair;
And Peace and Joy, a ſiſter pair:
And Kindneſs mild, their kindred Grace,
Whoſe brow ſerene complacence wears,
Whoſe hand her liberal bounty bears
O'er the vaſt range of animated ſpace !

Bleſt

Bleſt viſion! O for ever ſtay!

O far be Guilt and Pain away!

And yet, perhaps, with HIM, whoſe view

Looks at one glance creation through,

To general good our partial ill

Seems but a ſand upon the plain,

Seems but a drop amid the main,

And ſome wiſe unknown purpoſe may fulfil,

O D E   XXVII.

AFTER READING AKENSIDE'S POEMS.

––––––––

TO Fancy's view what vifions rife,
    Remote amid yon azure fkies!
  What Goddefs-form defcends in air?
  The Grecian Mufe, feverely fair!
  What Sage is he, to whom fhe deigns
  Her lyre of elevated ftrains?
  The Bard of Tyne—his mafter hand
  Awakes new mufic o'er the land;
  And much his voice of right and wrong
  Attempts to teach the unheeding throng.

    What mean thofe chryftal rocks ferene,
  Thofe laureate groves for ever green,

R

Thofe

Thofe Parian domes?—Sublime retreats,

Of Freedom's fons the happy feats!—

There dwell the Few who dared difdain

The luft of power and luft of gain;

The Patriot names of old renown'd,

And thofe in later ages found;

The Athenian, Spartan, Roman boaft,

The pride of Britain's fea-girt coaft!

But, oh! what darknefs intervenes!

But, oh! beneath, what different fcenes!

What Matron fhe, to grief refign'd,

Befide that ruin'd arch reclin'd?

Her fons, who once fo well could wield

The warrior-fpear, the warrior-fhield,

A turban'd Ruffian's fcourge conftrains

To toil on defolated plains!—

And She who leans that column nigh,

Where trampled arms and eagles lie;

Whofe

Whofe veil effays her blufh to hide,

Who checks the tear that haftes to glide ?

A mitred Prieft's oppreffive fway

She fees her drooping race obey :

Their vines unprun'd, their fields untill'd,

Their ftreets with want and mifery fill'd.

   And who is She, the Martial Maid

Along that cliff fo carelefs laid,

Whofe brow fuch laugh unmeaning wears,

Whofe eye fuch infolence declares,

Whofe tongue defcants, with fcorn fo vain,

On flaves of Ebro or of Seine ?

What griefly Churl*, what Harlot bold†,

Behind her, chains enormous hold ?

Tho' Virtue's warning voice be near,

Alas, fhe will not, will not hear !

And now fhe finks in fleep profound,

And now they bind her to the ground.

      * Avarice.   † Luxury.

           O what

O D E XXVII.

O what is He, his ghaftly form,

So half obfcur'd in cloud and ftorm,

Swift ftriding on*?—beneath his ftrides

Proud Empire's firmeft bafe fubfides;

Behind him dreary waftes remain,

Oblivion's dark chaotic reign !

* Ruin.

THE

MEXICAN PROPHECY:

AN ODE.

DE SOLIS, in his Hiſtory of the Conqueſt of Mexico, informs us, that, on the approach of Cortez to the neighbourhood of that city, the Emperor Motezuma ſent a number of magicians to attempt the deſtruction of the Spaniſh army. As the forcerers were practiſing their incantations, a dæmon appeared to them in the form of their idol Tlcatlepuca, and foretold the fall of the Mexican empire. On this legend is founded the following Poem. The conqueſt of Mexico was undertaken from motives of avarice, and accompanied with circumſtances of cruelty; but it produced the ſubverſion of a tyrannical government, and the abolition of a deteſtable religion of horrid rites and human ſacrifices.

Warriors! let the Wretches live!
Christians! pity and forgive!

MEXICAN PROPHECY.

FROM Cholula's hoftile plain *,

   Left her treacherous legions flain,

Left her temples all in flame,

CORTES' conquering army came.

High on Chalco's ftormy fteep

Shone their phalanx broad and deep;

High the Hifpanian banner rais'd,

Bore the Crofs in gold emblaz'd †.

Thick the gleaming fpears appear'd,

Loud the neighing fteeds were heard;

Flafh'd the mufquets lightnings round,

Roll'd their thunders o'er the ground,

---

* Cholula was a large city, not far diftant from Mexico. The inhabitants were in league with the Mexicans; and after profefling friendfhip for the Spaniards, endeavoured to furprife and deftroy them.

† The device on Cortes's ftandard was the Sign of the Crofs. —Vide De Solis.

     Echo'd

Echo'd from a thoufand caves,

Down to Tenuftitan's waves * ; —

Spacious lake, that far below

Bade its lucid level flow :

There the ever-funny fhore

Groves of palm and coco bore ;

Maize-fields rich, favannas green,

Stretch'd around, with towns between.

Tacubà, Tezeùco fair,

Rear'd their fhining roofs in air ;

Mexico's imperial pride

Glitter'd 'midft the glaffy tide,

Bright with gold, with filver bright,

Dazzling, charming all the fight †.

From their poft the war-worn band

Raptur'd view'd the happy land :

* Tenuftitan, otherwife Tenuchtitlan, the ancient name of the Lake of Mexico.

† The Spanifh hiftorians affert, that the walls and houfes of the Indian cities were compofed of a peculiar kind of glittering ftone or plafter, which at a diftance refembled filver.

'Hafte

‘ Hafte to victory, hafte to eafe,

‘ Mark the fpot that gives us thefe !’

On the exulting heroes ftrode,

Shunn’d the fmooth infidious road,

Shunn’d the rock’s impending fhade,

Shunn’d the expecting ambufcade *.

Deep within a gloomy wood

Motezume’s magicians ftood :

Tlcatlepuca’s horrid form,

God of famine, plague, and ftorm,

High on magic ftones they rais’d;

Magic fires before him blaz’d ;

Round the lurid flames they drew,

Flames whence fteams of fulphur flew ;

---

* The Indians had blocked up the ufual road to Mexico, and
opened another broader, and fmooth at the entrance, but which
led among rocks and precipices, where they had placed parties
in ambufh. Cortes difcovered the ftratagem, and ordered his
troops to remove the obftructions. Being afked by the Mexican
ambaffadors the reafon of this procedure, he replied, that the
Spaniards always chofe to encounter difficulties.

There,

There, while bleeding victims smok'd,

Thus his aid they loud invok'd:

   ‘ Minister supreme of ill,

‘ Prompt to punish, prompt to kill,

‘ MOTEZUMA asks thy aid !

‘ Foreign foes his realms invade;

‘ Vengeance on the strangers shed,

‘ Mix them instant with the dead!

‘ By thy temple's sable floor,

‘ By thy altar stain'd with gore,

‘ Stain'd with gore and strew'd with bones,

‘ Echoing shrieks, and echoing groans !

‘ Vengeance on the strangers shed,

‘ Mix them instant with the dead !’

  ORDAZ heard, VELASQUEZ heard—

Swift their fauchions' blaze appear'd;

ALVARADO rushing near,

Furious rais'd his glittering spear;

                Calm,

Calm, Olmedo mark'd the fcene*,

Calm he mark'd, and ftepp'd between:

‘ Vain their rites and vain their prayer,

‘ Weak attempts beneath your care;

‘ Warriors! let the wretches live!

‘ Chriftians! pity, and forgive!’

Sudden darknefs o'er them fpread,

Glow'd the woods with dufky red;

Vaft the Idol's ftature grew,

Look'd his face of ghaftly hue,

Frowning rage, and frowning hate,

Angry at his nation's fate;

Fierce his fiery eyes he roll'd,

Thus his tongue the future told;

Cortes' veterans paus'd to hear,

Wondering all, tho' void of fear:

 ‘ Mourn, devoted city, mourn!

 ‘ Mourn, devoted city, mourn!

---

* Bartholeme de Olmedo, chaplain to Cortes: he feems to have been a man of enlarged ideas, much prudence, moderation, and humanity.

       ‘ Doom'd

' Doom'd for all thy crimes to know

' Scenes of battle, fcenes of woe !

' Who is he—O fpare the fight !—

' Rob'd in gold, with jewels bright ?

' Hark ! he deigns the crowd to call ;

' Chiefs and warriors proftrate fall *.

' Reverence now to fury yields ;

' Strangers o'er him fpread your fhields !

' Thick the darts, the arrows, fly ;

' Haplefs Monarch ! he muft die !

' Mark the folemn funeral ftate

' Paffing thro' the weftern gate !

' Chàpultèqua's cave contains

' Mighty MOTEZUME's remains.

' Ceafe the ftrife ! alas, 'tis vain !

' Myriads throng Otumba's plain ;

---

* Motezuma, who was refident in the Spanifh quarters when they were attacked by the Mexicans, propofed fhewing himfelf to the people, in order to appeafe the tumult. At his firft appearance, he was regarded with veneration, which was foon exchanged for rage, to the effects whereof he fell a victim.

' Wide

' Wide their feathery crefts they wave,

' All the ftrong and all the brave *.

' Gleaming glory thro' the fkies,

' See the Imperial ftandard flies !

' Down by force refiftlefs torn;

' Off in haughty triumph borne.

' Slaughter heaps the vale with dead,

' Fugitives the mountains fpread.

    ' Mexico, 'tis thine to know

' More of battle, more of woe !—

' Bright in arms the ftranger train

' O'er thy caufeways move again.

' Bend the bow, the fhaft prepare,

' Join the breaftplate's folds with care;

---

* Cortes, in his retreat from Mexico, after the death of Mo-
tezuma, was followed and furrounded by the whole collective
force of the empire, in the plains of Otumba. After repelling
the attacks of his enemies, on every fide, with indefatigable va-
lour, he found himfelf overpowered by numbers; when, making
one defperate effort, with a few felect friends, he feized the im-
perial ftandard, killed the general, and routed the army.

' Raife the facrificial fire,

' Bid the captive youths expire *;

' Wake the facred trumpet's breath,

' Pouring anguifh, pouring death †;

' Troops from every ftreet repair,

' Clofe them in the fatal fnare;

' Valiant as they are, they fly,

' Here they yield, and there they die.

  ' Ceafe the ftrife! 'tis fruitlefs all,

' Mexico at laft muft fall!

' Lo! the dauntlefs band return,

' Furious for the fight they burn!

' Lo! auxiliar nations round,

' Crowding o'er the darken'd ground!

---

* De Solis relates, that the Mexicans facrificed to their idols a number of Spaniards, whom they had taken prifoners, and whofe cries and groans were diftinctly heard in the Spanifh camp, exciting fentiments of horror and revenge in their furviving companions.

† The above author obferves, that the Sacred Trumpet of the Mexicans was fo called, becaufe it was not permitted to any but the priefts to found it; and that only when they denounced war, and animated the people on the part of their gods.

' Corfes

7

‘ Corſes fill thy trenches deep;

‘ Down thy temple's lofty ſteep

‘ See thy prieſts, thy princes thrown—

‘ Hark ! I hear their parting groan !

‘ Blood thy Lake with crimſon dyes,

‘ Flames from all thy domes ariſe !

  ‘ What are thoſe that round thy ſhore

‘ Launch thy troubled waters o'er ?

‘ Swift canoes that from the fight

‘ Aid their vanquiſh'd monarch's flight;

‘ Ambuſh'd in the reedy ſhade,

‘ Them the ſtranger barks invade;

‘ Soon thy lord a captive bends,

‘ Soon thy far-fam'd empire ends * ;

‘ Otomèca ſhares thy ſpoils,

‘ Tlàſcalà in triumph ſmiles †.

* When the Spaniards had forced their way to the centre of
Mexico, Guatimozin, the reigning emperor, endeavoured to
eſcape in his canoes acroſs the Lake; but was purſued and taken
priſoner by Garcia de Holguin, captain of one of the Spaniſh
brigantines.

† The Otomies were a fierce, ſavage nation, never thoroughly
ſubdued by the Mexicans. Tlaſcala was a powerful neighbour-
ing republic, the rival of Mexico.

                                ‘ Mourn,

' Mourn, devoted city, mourn!

' Mourn, devoted city, mourn!

  ' Ceafe your boaft, O ftranger band,

' Conquerors of my fallen land!

' Avarice ftrides your van before,

' Phantom meagre, pale, and hoar!

' Difcord follows, breathing flame,

' Still oppofing claim to claim †;

' Kindred Dæmons hafte along!

' Hafte, avenge my country's wrong!'

Ceas'd the voice with dreadful founds,

Loud as tides that burft their bounds;

Roll'd the form in fmoke away,

Amaz'd on earth th' exorcifts lay;

Pondering on the dreadful lore,

Their courfe the Iberians downward bore;

Their helmets glittering o'er the vale,

And wide their enfigns fluttering in the gale.

---

† Alluding to the diffenfions which enfued among the Spa-
niards, after the conqueft of America.

EPISTLES.

The Grotto at Amwell.

EPISTLE I.

THE GARDEN.

TO A FRIEND,

FROM Whitby's rocks fteep rifing o'er the main,

From Efka's vales, or Ewecot's lonely plain,

Say, rove thy thoughts to Amwell's diftant bow'rs,

To mark how pafs thy Friend's fequefter'd hours?

'Perhaps,' think'ft thou, 'he feeks his pleafing fcenes

'Of winding walks, fmooth lawns, and fhady greens:

'Where China's willow hangs its foliage fair,

'And Po's tall poplar waves its top in air,

S 2

'And

‘ And the dark maple fpreads its umbrage wide,

‘ And the white bench adorns the bafon fide;

‘ At morn reclin’d, perhaps, he fits to view

‘ The bank’s neat flope, the water’s filver hue.

   ‘ Where, ’midft thick oaks, the fubterraneous way

‘ To the arch’d grot admits a feeble ray;

‘ Where gloffy pebbles pave the varied floors,

‘ And rough flint-walls are deck’d with fhells and ores,

‘ And filvery pearls, fpread o’er the roofs on high,

‘ Glimmer like faint ftars in a twilight fky;

‘ From noon’s fierce glare, perhaps, he pleas’d retires,

‘ Indulging mufings which the place infpires.

   ‘ Now where the airy octagon afcends,

‘ And wide the profpect o’er the vale extends,

‘ ’Midft evening’s calm, intent perhaps he ftands,

‘ And looks o’er all that length of fun-gilt lands,

‘ Of bright green paftures, ftretch’d by rivers clear,

‘ And willow groves, or ofier iflands near.’

Alas,

Alas, my friend, how ftrangely men miftake,

Who guefs what others moft their pleafure make!

Thefe garden fcenes, which Fafhion o'er our plains

Spreads round the villas of our wealthy fwains,

Tho' Envy grudge, or Friendfhip wifh to fhare,

They claim but little of their owners' care.

For me, my groves not oft my fteps invite,

And far lefs oft they fail to offend my fight:

In vain the fenna waves its gloffy gold,

In vain the ciftus' fpotted flowers unfold,

In vain the acacia's fnowy bloom depends,

In vain the fumach's fcarlet fpike afcends,

In vain the woodbine's fpicy tufts difclofe,

And green flopes redden with the fhedding rofe:

Thefe neat-fhorn hawthorns ufelefs verdant bound,

This long ftraight walk, that pool's unmeaning

    round,

Thefe fhort-curv'd paths that twift beneath the trees,

Difguft the eye, and make the whole difpleafe.

'No

' No fcene like this,' I fay, ' did Nature raife,

' Brown's fancy form, or Walpole's * judgment

  ' praife;

' No prototype for this did I furvey

' In Woollett's landfcapes †, or in Mason's lay.'

But might thy genius, Friend, an Eden frame,

Profufe of beauty, and fecure from blame;

Where round the lawn might wind the varied way,

Now loft in gloom, and now with profpect gay;

Now fcreen'd with clumps of green, for wintry bow'rs;

Now edg'd with funny banks, for fummer flow'rs;

Now led by chryftal lakes with lilies dreft,

Or where light temples court the ftep to reft—

Time's gradual change, or Tempeft's fudden rage,

There with thy peace perpetual war would wage.

 * See Mr. Walpole's ingenious Hiftory of the Modern Tafte in Gardening, at the end of the Fourth Volume of his Anecdotes of Painting.

 † The above-named excellent Artift, feveral years ago, drew and engraved a number of beautiful views in fome of our moft celebrated modern gardens.

That

That tyrant oak, whofe arms fo far o'ergrow,

Shades fome poor fhrub that pines with drought below;

Thefe rampant elms, thofe hazels branching wide,

Crowd the broad pine, the fpiry larix hide.

That lilac brow, where May's unfparing hand

Bade one vaft fwell of purple bloom expand,

Soon paft its prime, fhews figns of quick decay,

The naked ftem, and fcanty-cover'd fpray.

Fierce Boreas calls, and Ruin waits his call;

Thy fair catalpa's broken branches fall;

Thy foft magnolia mourns her blafted green,

And blighted laurel's yellowing leaves are feen.

But Difcontent alone, thou'lt fay, complains

For ill fuccefs, where none perfection gains:

True is the charge; but from that tyrant's fway

What art, what power, can e'er redeem our day?

To me, indeed, fhort eafe he fometimes yields,

When my lone walk furrounds the rural fields;

There no paſt errors of my own upbraid,

No time, no wealth, expended unrepaid :

There Nature dwells, and throws profuſe around

Each paſtoral fight and every paſtoral found ;

From Spring's green copſe, that pours the cuckoo's
　　　　ſtrain,

And evening bleatings of the fleecy train,

To Autumn's yellow field, and clamorous horn *

That wakes the ſlumbering harveſters at morn.

There Fancy too, with fond delighted eyes,

Sees o'er the ſcene ideal people riſe ;

There calm Contentment, in his cot reclin'd,

Hears the grey poplars whiſper in the wind ;

---

* There is a cuſtom, frequent in many parts of England, of
calling the harveſt-men to and from work by the found of a horn.
This practice, as well as that of the Harveſt-Shouting, ſeems
much on the decline. The latter could boaſt its origin from high
antiquity, as appears from that beautiful ſtroke of Faſtern Po-
etry, Iſaiah, chap. xvi : " I will water thee with my tears, O
" Heſhbon and Elealeh ; for the ſhouting for thy ſummer fruits,
" and for thy harveſt, is fallen !"

There

There Love's sweet song adown the echoing dale

To Beauty's ear conveys the tender tale;

And there Devotion lifts his brow to Heaven,

With grateful thanks for many a blessing given.

Thus oft thro' Maylan's shady lane I stray,

Trace Rushgreen's paths, or Postwood's winding way;

Thus oft to Eastfield's airy height I haste;

(All well-known spots thy feet have frequent trac'd!)

While Memory, as my sight around I cast,

Suggests the pleasing thought of moments past;

Or Hope, amid the future, forms again

The dream of bliss Experience broke in vain.

EPISTLE II.

WINTER AMUSEMENTS IN THE COUNTRY.

TO A FRIEND IN LONDON.

———————

WHILE Thee, my Friend, the City's ſcenes
  detain,—

The chearful ſcenes where Trade and Pleaſure reign;

Where glittering ſhops their varied ſtores diſplay,

And paſſing thouſands crowd the public way;

Where Painting's forms and Muſic's ſounds delight,

And Faſhion's frequent novelties invite,

And Converſation's ſober ſocial hours

Engage the mind, and elevate its powers—

Far different ſcenes for us the country yields,

Deſerted roads and unfrequented fields:

Yet deem not, lonely as they are, that theſe

Boaſt nought to charm the eye, the ear to pleaſe.

Tho'

Tho' here the Tyrant Winter holds command,

And bids rude tempeſts deſolate the land;

Sometimes the Sun extends his chearing beam,

And all the landſcape caſts a golden gleam:

Clear is the ſky, and calm and ſoft the air,

And thro' thin miſt each objeƈt looks more fair.

   Then, where the villa rears its ſheltering grove,

Along the ſouthern lawn 'tis ſweet to rove:

There dark green pines, behind, their boughs extend,

And bright ſpruce firs like pyramids aſcend,

And round their tops, in many a pendent row,

Their ſcaly cones of ſhining auburn ſhow;

There the broad cedar's level branches ſpread,

And the tall cypreſs lifts its ſpiry head;

With alaternus ilex interweaves,

And laurels mix their gloſſy oval leaves;

And gilded holly crimſon fruit diſplays,

And white viburnum * o'er the border ſtrays.

* _Viburnum._ That well-known beautiful flowering evergreen, commonly called Lauruſtinus.

Where

Where thefe from ftorms the fpacious greenhoufe
  fcreen,
Ev'n now the eye beholds a flow'ry fcene;
There chryftal fafhes ward the injurious cold,
And rows of benches fair exotics hold;
Rich plants, that Afric's funny cape fupplies,
Or o'er the ifles of either India rife.

 While ftrip'd geranium fhows its tufts of red,
And verdant myrtles grateful fragrance fhed;
A moment ftay to mark the vivid bloom,
A moment ftay to catch the high perfume,
And then to rural fcenes—Yon path, that leads
Down the fteep bourn and 'crofs the level meads,
Soon mounts the opponent hill, and foon conveys
To where the farm its pleafing group difplays:
The ruftic manfion's form, antiquely fair;
The yew-hedg'd garden, with its grafs-plat fquare;
The barn's long ridge, and doors expanded wide;
The ftable's ftraw-clad eves and clay-built fide;

        The

The cartfhed's roof, of rough-hewn roundwood made,
And loofe on heads of old fere pollards laid;
The granary's floor that fmooth-wrought pofts fuftain,
Where hungry vermin ftrive to climb in vain;
And many an afh that wild around them grows,
And many an elm that fhelter o'er them throws.

Then round the moat we turn, with pales inclos'd,
And 'midft the orchard's trees in rows difpos'd,
Whofe boughs thick tufts of mifletoe adorn
With fruit of lucid white on joints of yellow borne.

Thence up the lane, romantic woods among,
Beneath old oaks with ivy overhung
(O'er their rough trunks the hairy ftalks intwine,
And on their arms the fable berries fhine):
Here oft the fight, on banks beftrewn with leaves,
The early primrofe' opening bud perceives;
And oft fteep dells or ragged cliffs unfold
The prickly furze with bloom of brighteft gold;
Here oft the red-breaft hops along the way,
And 'midft grey mofs explores his infect prey;

Or

Or the green woodſpite* flies with outcry ſhrill,

And delves the ſere bough with his ſounding bill;

Or the rous'd hare ſtarts ruſtling from the brake,

And gaudy jays inceſſant clamour make;

Or echoing hills return from ſtubbles nigh

The ſportſman's gun, and ſpaniel's yelping cry.

And now the covert ends in open ground,

That ſpreads wide views beneath us all around;

There turbid waters, edg'd with yellow reeds,

Roll thro' the ruſſet herd-forſaken meads;

There from the meads th' incloſures ſloping riſe,

And, 'midſt th' incloſures, duſky woodland lies;

While pointed ſpires and curling ſmokes, between,

Mark towns and vills and cottages unſeen.

And now,—for now the breeze and noontide ray

Clear the laſt remnants of the miſt away,—

Far, far o'er all extends the aching eye,

Where azure mountains mingle with the ſky:

* *Woodſpite.* The Green Woodpecker. —Vide Pennant's Bri-
tiſh Zoology, folio, p. 78.

To

To thefe the curious optic tube applied

Reveals each object diftance elfe would hide;

There feats or homefteads, plac'd in pleafant fhades,

Show   their   white   walls   and   windows   thro'   the
           glades;

There rears the hamlet church its hoary tow'r

(The clock's bright index points the paffing hour);

There green-rob'd huntfmen o'er the funny lawn

Lead home their beagles from the chace withdrawn,

And ploughs flow-moving turn the broad champaign,

And on fteep fummits feed the fleecy train.

But wintry months few days like thefe fupply,

And their few moments far too fwiftly fly:

Dank thaws, chill fogs, rough winds, and beating rain,

To fheltering rooms th' unwilling ftep detain;

Yet there, my Friend, fhall liberal Science find

Amufement various for th' inquiring mind.

While Hiftory's hand her fanguine record brings,

With woes of nations fraught, and crimes of kings;

Plague thins the ſtreet, and Famine blaſts the plain,

War wields his ſword, Oppreſſion binds his chain;

Curioſity purſues the unfolding tale,

Which Reaſon blames, and Pity's tears bewail.

   While Fancy's powers the eventful novel frame,

And Virtue's care directs its conſtant aim;

As Fiction's pen domeſtic life portrays,

Its hopes and fears and joys and griefs diſplays;

By GRANDISON'S or CLINTON'S * ſtory mov'd,

We read delighted, and we riſe improv'd.

   Then with bold Voyagers our thought explores

Vaſt tracts of ocean and untrodden ſhores;

Now views rude climes, where ice-rocks drear aſpire,

Or red volcanos ſhoot their ſtreams of fire:

Now ſeeks ſweet iſles, where lofty palm-groves wave,

And cany banks tranſlucent rivers lave;

Where Plenty's gifts luxuriant load the ſoil,

And Eaſe repoſes, charm'd with Beauty's ſmile.

   * Vide The Fool of Quality, a well-known novel, by Mr.
Henry Brooke, author of Guſtavus Vaſa, &c.

                       Such,

Such, haplefs Cook*! amid the fouthern main,

Rofe thy Ta-heitè's peaks and flowery plain;—

Why, daring Wanderer! quit that blifsful land,

To feek new dangers on a barbarous ftrand?

Why doom'd, fo long efcap'd from ftorms and foes,

Upon that ftrand thy dying eyes to clofe;

Remote each place by habit render'd dear,

Nor Britifh friends nor Otaheitean near?

Nor lefs than books the Engraver's works invite,

Where paft and diftant come before the fight;

Where, all the Painter's lively tints convey'd,

The fkilful Copyift gives in light and fhade:

While faithful views the profpect's charms difplay,

From coaft to coaft, and town to town, we ftray;

While faithful portraits human features trace,

We gaze delighted on the fpeaking face;

Survey the port that bards and heroes bore,

Or mark the fmiles that high-born beauties wore.

* This celebrated Circumnavigator, after furmounting nume-
rous difficulties, and efcaping many dangers, was at length flain
by the inhabitants of Owhyhee, a little ifland in the Pacific Ocean.

Ceafe

Ceafe thefe to pleafe ? Philofophy attends

With arts where knowledge with diverfion blends;

The Sun's vaft fyftem in a model fhows;

Bids the clear lens new forms to fight expofe;

Conftructs machines, whofe wond'rous powers declare

The effects of light, and properties of air;

With whirling globes excites electric fires,

And all their force and all their ufe inquires.

O Nature! how immenfe thy fecret ftore,

Beyond what ev'n a PRIESTLEY can explore!

Such, Friend, the employments may his time divide,

Whom rural fhades from fcenes of bufinefs hide;

While o'er his ear unnotic'd glide away

The noife and nonfenfe of the paffing day *!

---

* A fhort Epiftle, partly on the fame plan as the foregoing,
was, fome years ago, inadvertently fuffered to appear in a Col-
lection of Poems, by Several Hands, publifhed by G. Pearch.
—Such lines of that Piece, as were thought worth prefervation,
are here retained.

AN

ESSAY

ON

PAINTING.

The Author had conceived a defign of writing a pretty extenfive Poem on the fubject of Painting, long before Mr. Hayley's ingenious " Poetical Epiftle to an Eminent Painter" appeared. That performance anticipated and precluded part of his intended Work, but feemed not to render the fuppreffion of the following Lines neceffary.

A N

ESSAY on PAINTING.

TO A YOUNG ARTIST.

———————

FROM funny Adria's fea-furrounded towers,
 From Tyber's vales and Arno's viny bowers,
The Mufe of Painting feeks Britannia's plain,
And leads to Thames's bank her favourite train:
There, where a nation's wealth her dome has plac'd,
With her kind Sifter's † Attic beauties grac'd,
She, like the Spring, as liberal and as gay,
Bids her rich hand its annual ftores difplay;
And mimic Being glowing round the walls,
From fcene to fcene the rapt attention calls.

† Architecture.

There,

There, where the Public gives the palm of praiſe,

And only Merit to renown can raiſe,

Doubtleſs, my Friend, the juſt ambition 's thine

To ſee thy future works diſtinguiſh'd ſhine.

Hear then thy Poet's monitory lay,

That hints not uſeleſs may perchance convey:

No artiſt I, like Him of Gallia's ſhore *,

Whoſe pencil practis'd, ere he taught his lore;

Yet Taſte incites me others' works to view,

And riſk a judgment haply not untrue.

Were Painting's path my pleaſing road to fame,

The choice of ſubject much my care ſhould claim;

His graphic power he ſure but ill beſtows,

Who beſt a trifle's nice reſemblance ſhows.

'Tho' the rich tints ſo finely blended fall,

When carps and pheaſants deck the rural hall,

* C. A. Du Freſnoy, a well-known French Painter; author
of a Latin poem, De Arte Graphica.

That

That oft, like ZEUXIS' grapes, they fcarcely fail

To tempt to touch the feather or the fcale,—

Yet not ev'n ELMER's* fkill can make us prize

What every field or every pond fupplies;

Regret gives pain to view fuch wonderous art

Tried on no theme that interefts the heart.

The pride of Genius fhould thy hand reftrain

From all that Life's inferior ranks contain † ;

Thy confcious pallet ne'er its hues fhould fpare

To draw a fportfman's hound or racer's mare ;

Nor thy reluctant crayon ftoop to trace

A fool's dull eye, or villain's ill-mark'd face.

---

* The Author muft here once for all remark, that whatever he may fay refpecting the works of any Painter is folely the refult of impartial, though poffibly miftaken opinion. He cannot be mifled by friendfhip ; for, excepting a flight acquaintance with thefe amiable characters, Mr. Weft and Mrs. Kauffman, he has not the pleafure of knowing any Artift whofe name he has taken the liberty to mention.

† This is meant only of fuch objects, when confidered as the principal fubject of a picture. Almoft every clafs of animals may be occafionally introduced as ornaments in landfcape, and often in hiftory.

But

But deem not Portrait's gifts I mean to

    flight,—

Portrait, the fource of many a pure delight!

When Bards' or Sages' works our wifhes fire

To fee their forms whofe minds we there admire,

The featur'd canvas full to view difplays

Reafon's deep calm or Fancy's glowing rays.

When Beauty's charms their varied graces wear,

Love's gentle fmile, or Mirth's vivacious air,

The pleafing image ftrikes remoteft climes,

And goes unalter'd down to diftant times.

When Death's relentlefs hand in duft has laid

The fchool-companion, or the firft-lov'd maid;

The father kind, with filial awe rever'd;

The tender mother, by her cares endear'd;

When from our arms the darling child is torn,

Or when the hufband or the wife we mourn—

As on their picture many a glance we caft,

Remembrance wanders to the vanifh'd paft;

                              Our

Our thoughts o'er numberlefs minutiæ roll,

And pain-mix'd pleafure folaces the foul.

To Portrait's ftudy fhould thy choice incline,

Ev'n there to aim at excellence be thine;

And ftrive to reach the point that few can gain,

Preferve the likenefs, yet the fpirit retain.

Of Landfcape's province wide extends the range,

From the deep vale and humble rural grange,

To Cambrian heaths fublimely brown and bare *,

Or Alpine ice-points glittering white in air:

And not from Nature only fhe defigns,

But different parts of different fcenes combines;

Or new creations of her own fhe forms,

Illumes with funfhine, or involves in ftorms †.

* That celebrated artift, Mr. Wilfon, has painted a fet of beautiful Views from Nature, in different parts of Wales.

† Thefe circumftances, termed by the Painters *Accidents of Nature*, often agreeably diverfify landfcape.

Familiar

Familiar profpects would thy hand beftow?

Mark what our hay-fields and our hop-grounds fhow;

Where in neat rows the ruffet cocks are feen,

Or from tall poles depend feftoons of green;

And long ftraight paths in perfpective extend,

And yellow fandhills clofe behind afcend *.

Nor fweeter contraft fure can meet the eye

Than village lanes in vernal months fupply,

When amber clouds, in fky of foft bright blue,

Hang o'er the copfe juft crown'd with verdure
    new;

Or where the orchard's fun-gilt branches fpread

Their bloom of white or faintly-blufhing red.

The faireft fcenes, when peopled, look more fair,

But thefe to people afks peculiar care:

We wifh not here for VIRGIL's claffic fwains,

Nor Dryad nymphs light tripping o'er the plains;

* For this imagery the Author is indebted to Mr. Walpole,
who, in his Anecdotes of Painting, vol. iv. p. 65, propofes our
hay-fields and hop-grounds as new fubjects of landfcape.

Nor

Nor yet the grinning Hobbinols of GAY,

Nor cottage Marians in their torn array :

The ruſtic life, in every varied place,

Can boaſt its few of beauty and of grace ;

From them ſelect the forms that moſt may pleaſe,

And clothe with ſimple elegance and eaſe :

Such forms in SMITH's * delightful ſpots we prize,

And ſuch in SANDBY's pleaſant fields ariſe.

   The obſervant Artiſt much from travel gains ;

Increaſe of knowledge well rewards his pains.

Now his pleas'd eye o'er Tuſcan proſpects roves,

Their ſunny corn-fields and their cypreſs groves ;

Their roads, where ſports from tree to tree the vine,

And thro' broad leaves its chryſtal cluſters ſhine † ;

Their white Caſines, with olive groves around ;

And glittering cliffs with towns and caſtles crown'd.

  * The late Mr. George Smith of Chicheſter.

  † The hedgerow trees in Tuſcany are covered with vines.—
Vide Smollet's Travels, vol. ii. p. 46.

Now

Now his pleas'd ſtep a wider circuit tries,

Where Nile's vaſt flood on Egypt's level lies ;

While 'midſt the tide tall palms their tops uprear,

And cauſeways broad and cities fair appear *.

Now Indian climes he eaſt or weſt explores,

Quits the dull factory and the ſandy ſhores †,

Climbs craggy hills, pervades romantic woods,

Or winds along the cataracts of the floods ;

Thro' beaſts and birds and inſects, fruits and flow'rs,

In ſhape and colour all diſtinct from ours ;

Or ſtrays o'er iſles that ſpicy yales unfold,

'Midſt ſkies of glory and 'midſt ſeas of gold ;

Such ſkies, ſuch ſeas, as HODGES' pencil drew,

And round the rocks of Ulitea threw ‡.

* Vide Rollin's Ancient Hiſtory, 18mo. vol. i. p. 22.

† Several of our Artiſts have attended to this circumſtance of foreign ſcenery. The ingenious Mr. George Robertſon has painted ſeveral fine romantic Views in Jamaica, which have been engraved.

‡ Several beautiful Landſcapes, taken in different parts of the New Diſcovered Iſlands, by Mr. Hodges, who attended Captain Cook in one of his Voyages, muſt be well remembered by thoſe who attend the annual Exhibitions of the Royal Academy.

Whate'er

Whate'er we copy, or whate'er we feign,

Thro' all the piece one character fhould reign :

When CLAUDE's bright morn on Mola's precincts

    dawns,

What fweet quiefcence marks the groves and lawns !

How calm his herds among the ruins graze !

How calm his curious peafant ftands to gaze* !

When bold SALVATOR under turbid fkies

Bids his fcath'd hills and blafted trees arife,

Behind wild rocks bids his wild ftreams be loft,

And from vaft cliffs fhews broken fragments toft ;

'Midft them no fhepherds lead their flocks along,

Nor village maidens feem to tune their fong ;

But folemn augurs flights of birds furvey,

Or ftern-eyed robbers wait the paffing prey † .

---

  * Vide a beautiful Engraving, by Vivarez, from a capital
Picture of Claude Lorrain, called the Morning, in which he in-
troduces himfelf drawing an antique temple on the banks of the
Tyber, between Ponte Mola and Rome.

  † Vide Salvator Rofa's Landfcapes, engraved by Goupy.
See alfo Sir Jofhua Reynolds's Difcourfes, p. 175.

In Rubens' foreſt, when the wounded boar,

Plung'd in the ſtream, attempts the further ſhore,

How the fierce dogs retard his aukward ſpeed !

How the fierce hunters urge the ſtraining ſteed !

And eager one the winged arrow ſends,

And one firm-fix'd the expectant ſpear protends *,

To Hiſtory's group, where paſſion'd thought expreſt

Strikes kindred feelings on the gazer's breaſt, —

To Hiſtory's group, the epic of thy art,

Proceed we now, and what we can, impart.

The mighty Maſters of Italian name

All Rome, all Florence, and Bologna claim ;

Whoſe freſco forms ſtill animate their walls,

Whoſe living canvas decks their domes and halls :

What various powers for theſe their glory won,

And what of theirs to chuſe, and what to ſhun,

* Vide Rubens's Landſcape of boar-hunting, engraved by Bolſwert.

Illuſtrious

Illuftrious REYNOLDS much in profe has told,

And more my verfe pretends not to unfold.

Thefe ftill thy ftudy but with caution make,

Nor prize the picture for the Painter's fake;

RAFFAELLE himfelf, beneath himfelf oft fell,

And meaner hands' beft works his worft excel *.

'Tis General Nature, in thy art and mine,

Muft give our fame in future times to fhine:

Sublime and pathos, like the Sun's fix'd flame,

Remain, and pleafe thro' every age the fame;

Humour's light fhapes, like vapours in the fky,

Rife, pafs, and vary, and for ever fly:

HOGARTH and SWIFT, if living, might deplore

Half their keen jokes, that now are jokes no more.

* For this affertion the Author has the higheft authority,
viz. that of Sir Jofhua Reynolds. " I have no defire," fays he,
" to degrade Raffaelle from the high rank he defervedly holds;
" but, in comparing him with himfelf, he does not appear to me
" to be the fame man in Oil as in Frefco."—Difcourfes, p. 165.

What

What Truth's rich page of real event fupplies,

What Fancy's powers of fabled act devife,

Before thee lie—but where the field fo wide,

There Judgment's hand Selection's ftep muft guide.

To Horror's forms the mind averfion feels,

To SPANIOLET's* flay'd faints and torturing wheels;

Nor praife for naufeous images we win,

For SPENSER's Error, or for MILTON's Sin.

Mythology, that Greek enchantrefs, long

Has reign'd the idol of the painting throng:

But Reafon's thought difdains OVIDIAN dreams

Abfurd, of nymphs transform'd to trees and ftreams;

And Virtue HOMER's wanton gods abhors,

With all their lewd amours and all their idle wars.

* *Spaniolet.* Giofeppe Ribera, a native of Valencia in Spain.
He was noted for painting horrid fubjects; fuch as Prometheus
with the Vulture feeding on his liver; Ixion tortured on the
wheel; and St. Bartholomew with the fkin flayed from his body.
—Vide Dryden's Tranflation of Frefnoy, p. 352.

The

The Battle's conflicts ample scope bestow
The effects of fury, fear, and pain to show;
As different features these unlike express,
The contrast's force affects us more or less.
But here Confusion holds his crowded reign,
And the tir'd eye attempts to rest in vain;
And o'er thè scene Humanity complains,
Where mangled corfes lie, and blood the land
  distains.
When in the fore-ground kings or generals stand,
Direct the attack, or head the charging band,
Their graceful forms we unconcern'd survey,
Who fight for conquest, or who fight for pay:
Nor in their postures can there much be prais'd,
Their pistols levell'd, or their fauchions rais'd;
And to dull sameness here so oft we fall,
That who beholds one piece, beholds them all.
 But War's dire field, not all confin'd to these,
Affords us often incidents that please:

U

For oft the Hiftorian's, oft the Poet's art,

Can win our wifhes on fome hero's part;

His country nam'd, his place and parents known,

Our bufy thought his perils makes its own.

To fierce PELIDES, 'midft Scamander's waves,

When young LYCAON's voice for pity craves *;

The Chief's ftern brow, and lance fufpended high,

The Youth's bent knee and deprecating eye,

Not WEST's rich pencil need difdain to trace,

Or ROMNEY's ftroke with glowing colours grace.

When DITHYRAMBUS, on Oëta's plain,

Mourns the brave Perfian whom his hand has flain,

Nor marks his danger from the approaching foe,

Nor his bold friend prepar'd to ward the blow;

---

* Vide the Iliad, book xxi.--This ftory of Lycaon is perhaps one of the moft affecting paffages in the whole Poem. Vide Pope's Note, vol. v. p. 208. of his Tranflation. The countenance of Achilles, at the moment when the death of Patroclus, occurring to his thought, determined him to kill Lycaon, would afford a fine expreffion :

    " Talk not of life or ranfom, he replies;
    " Patroclus dead, whoever meets me dies."

In

In one what grief, in one what vengeful rage,

In one what ardour, might the fight engage*!

The gentle KAUFFMAN's traits can beſt declare

The ſentimental feelings of the Fair,

When ſoft ERMINIA in the ſylvan ſhade

Leaves TANCRED's name on every tree diſplay'd †;

Or kind LOUISA pens the friendly ſcroll,

To ſooth the mournful ſiſter of her ſoul ‡.

* Vide Leonidas, book viii. l. 355.
    " He ended, ruſhing furious on the Greek,
    " Who, while his gallant enemy expir'd,
    " While Hyperanthes tenderly receiv'd
    " The laſt embraces of his gaſping friend,
    " Stood nigh reclin'd in ſadneſs on his ſhield,
    " And in the pride of victory repin'd.
    " Unmark'd his foe approach'd. But forward
        " ſprung
    " Diomedon. Before the Theſpian youth
    " Aloft he rais'd his targe——— "

† Vide Taſſo's Jeruſalem Delivered.

‡ See Emma Corbett, an intereſting novel, by Mr. S. I. Pratt, Vol. i. Letter 34.

           The

The fame fkill'd hand more ftrong expreffion tries,

At Edward's feet when Woodville's daughter lies*;

Or, 'midft the admiring weeping train around,

Fond Eleanora fucks the poifon'd wound †.

Delightful Artift!—Grace her pencil guides,

And Delicacy o'er its ftroke prefides!

The immortal Swans, appointed to redeem

Genius and Worth from Lethe's filent ftream,

Pleas'd with their charge fhall bear her medall'd name

To the fair Prieftefs of the fane of Fame ‡.

Such tender fubjeêts, if thy choice they gain,

Enough for thee as yet untouch'd remain.

---

* See the ftory of Elizabeth Grey, daughter of Sir Richard Woodville, fuing to Edward IV. for reftitution of her lands.— Rapin, vol. i. p. 601.

† The well-known ftory of Eleanor of Caftile, queen of Edward I., fucking the poifon from her hufband's arm, when he was wounded by an affaffin in Paleftine.

‡ See a Painting of Mrs. Kauffman's, from a paffage in Ariofto, where fwans are introduced bringing the names of ingenious perfons, infcribed on medals, to a nymph who depofits them in the Temple of Fame.

Now

Now from the page of RICHARDSON beſtow

On CLEMENTINA's face the lines of woe;

Or let ſweet HARRIET's livelier beauty wear

The ſoul-fraught eye and apprehenſive air;

Or draw the proud OLIVIA's rage-fluſh'd charms,

When the calm Hero ſeiz'd her deadly arms;

And paint that Hero, firm in trial prov'd,

Unaw'd by Danger, and by Vice unmov'd *.

To STERNE's ſoft Maniac let thy hand impart

The languid cheek, the look that pierc'd his heart,

When to her Virgin Saint the veſper ſong ſhe rais'd,

Or earneſt view'd him as he ſat and gaz'd †.

Mark,

* The Hiſtory of Sir Charles Grandiſon, vol. iv. p. 176. The interview between Grandiſon and Olivia, at the inſtant of his ſeizing her poniard, would make a noble picture. This work of Richardſon's abounds with fine ſituations. Brooke's Fool of Quality, and the Adventurer of Hawkeſworth, are alſo books worthy the peruſal of an artiſt who wiſhes for choice of intereſting incidents.

† This ſubject has been attempted by ſeveral ingenious artiſts, who have given very pleaſing figures; but perhaps none that convey the preciſe idea of Sterne. This author

being

Mark, if thou can'ft, Philanthropy divine,

That fwells the breaft and bids the features fhine,

When the tear gliftening ftarts from TOBY's eyes

Fix'd on the couch where poor LE FEVRE dies.

The Grecian claffics' venerable lore

I fee thee often diligent explore;

What HOMER's Mufe to Chian cities taught,

Or Pity's Prieft * to Athens' audience brought.

Methinks, now rifing from thy plaftic hand,

Troy's hoary Monarch fhall a fuppliant ftand;

To ftern ACHILLES all his griefs explain,

And afk his HECTOR's corfe, nor afk in vain †.

being mentioned, a trite obfervation muft be indulged, viz.
That there probably never was a more ftriking inftance of mif-
application of talents than in him. With fuperior powers for
the pathos, he chofe to defcend to ribaldry, that affronted the
tafte and corrupted the morals of the Public. What pity that the
gold had not been feparated from the drofs, and the latter con-
figned to that oblivion it fo richly merits!

  * Euripides; termed fo by Collins.

  † Vide the Iliad, book xxiv.

Now

Now Jove's kind Son to Thebes's forrowing King

Shall his reftor'd unknown Alcestis bring;

Admetus' eyes his anguifh'd thoughts declare,

And turn'd difgufted from the proffer'd Fair *.

The Dark Sublime of extra-natural fcenes

The vulgar magic's puerile rite demeans;

Where hags their caldrons fraught with toads prepare,

Or glide on broomfticks thro' the midnight air.

Chain'd on the rock let bold Prometheus lie,

And caft wild looks, upbraiding, to the fky †;

Bid Milton's Satan from the burning fteep

Call his wide legions, flumbering on the deep;

Or Camoens' Spirit of the Cape upraife,

And fhow him only by the lightning's blaze;

* Vide the Alceftis of Euripides. Hercules reftores to life Alceftis, the deceafed wife of Admetus, and brings her to her hufband, difguifed with a veil, and reprefented as a ftranger; whom Admetus, in the height of diftrefs for the lofs of his beloved confort, refufes to admit into his palace.

† See the Prometheus of Æfchylus.

U 4   Or

Or place fad Hosier's Ghoft amid the tide,

Where by the pale Moon anchor'd navies ride *.

O where is He, whofe thought fuch grandeur gave

To bold Fitzwalter and the barons brave,

When, rang'd in arms along their Thames's ftrand,

They fnatch'd their charter from a tyrant's hand † ?

Thro' all the fcenes his rapid ftroke beftow'd,

Rosa's wild grace and daring fpirit glow'd ;

In him—ah loft ere half his powers were fhown !—

Britain perhaps an Angelo had known !

Wouldft thou his honours emulous purfue,

And give the Patriot Energy to view,—

Deep in the gloom of Dalecarlia's mine,

Bid Freedom's flame in Vasa's vifage fhine ‡ ;

---

* See that admirable fong, intitled Hofier's Ghoft; by the Author of Leonidas.

† Vide the late Mr. Mortimer's Picture of King John delivering Magna Charta to the Barons. That ingenious Artift's obvious powers of imagination promifed the attainment of a high degree of excellence in his profeffion.

‡ Brooke's Guftavus Vafa, act i. fc. 2. where Guftavus difcovers himfelf to Anderfon and Arnoldus in the copper-mines of Dalecarlia. See another fine fubject in the fame Tragedy, act iv. fcene xi.

The

The pafs of fam'd Thermopylæ difplay,

And Sparta's Monarch's port auguft pourtray *.

For Pontiffs and for Kings, the Painter's fkill

From Sacred Story toils their walls to fill;

Where'er we turn, its fubjects ftrike the eye,

And few untried are left for us to try.

Yet who has JEPTHAH's matchlefs woe expreft,

By his lov'd Daughter's fudden fight diftreft;

Or fhewn the Patriarchs, ftruck with wild amaze,

As on the Viceroy's hidden cup they gaze † ?

* Vide Leonidas, book x. where the Hero of the Poem re-
peats to the affembled council the meffage of Argeftes; while
Alpheus, at the fame inftant, brings news of the Perfians having
paffed the Upper Strait. This would make a noble picture;
the dauntlefs appearance of the Greeks might be well contrafted
with the fear and fhame of the ambaffador of Xerxes.—The
Banquet of Meliffa, Prieftefs of the Mufes, where Leonidas and
Æfchylus are fuppofed prefent, book vii. is another fine fubject.
Such pictures would hardly be popular; but to fome minds they
would afford fingular pleafure.

† The Author does not recollect feeing or hearing of any ce-
lebrated picture on thofe interefting fubjects, of Jepthah's re-
turn, and the difcovery of Jofeph's cup in the fack of Ben-
jamin.

Or

Or who, when IsRAEL's hofts on Edom's plain

Defpairing lie,—a thirft-afflicted train !—

Has bade the Prophet and his minftrel ftand,

And call new waters o'er the burning fand * ?

When DAVID's chiefs, with generous thought in-

fpir'd,

Bring the clear wave his fickening foul defir'd;

What dignity might to his act be given,

The pure libation pouring out to Heaven † !

No more of Theme; Defign muft now fucceed—

The mind's ftrong picture when we hear or read ‡,

Where every perfon finds his proper place,

And turn of attitude and turn of face :

---

* Vide 2 Kings, chap. iii.——This fubject would afford a
variety of noble expreffion in the different characters of the
Kings, the pious confidence of Jehofaphat, and the defponding
anxiety of Jehoram, the diftrefs of the foldiers, and the enthu-
fiafm of Elifha.   The ftreams of water might appear in the dif-
tance, feemingly vifible only to the Prophet, from his fituation.

† 2 Samuel, chap. xxiii.

‡ See Sir Jofhua Reynolds's Difcourfes, p. 104.

The

The Artiſt's powers in this muſt greatly fail,

Whoſe figures point not out at once his tale *.

When Lyſtra's crowd around the Apoſtles throng,

And joyful lead the victim ox along ;

Aſk we the cauſe, while He that cauſe explains,

Whoſe limb, late uſeleſs, ſtrength and uſe ob-
  tains † ?

When WEST's young Warrior, bleeding on the
  ground,

His mournful group of martial friends ſurround ;

Their gallant General inſtantly we know,

Their griefs, their cares, his life's importance ſhow ;

---

* " That compoſition muſt be defective, which cannot, to a
" careful obſerver, point out its own tendency ; and thoſe ex-
" preſſions muſt be either weak or falſe, which do not in
" ſome degree mark the intereſt of each actor in the
" drama."—Webb's Inquiry into the Beauties of Painting, pre-
face, p. 8.

† Vide Raffaelle's St. Paul and Barnabas at Lyſtra. For the
above obſervation and deſcription the Author is indebted to
the ingenious " Inquiry into the Beauties of Painting,"
p. 180.

Quebec's

Quebec's proud tower, the encountering troops be-
　　　tween,
In diſtant view diſcriminates the ſcene *.

　　As in the Drama all events ſhould tend
In courſe unbroken to the purpos'd end ;
So muſt the Picture's buſineſs ſtill maintain
The ſame connective unity of train.
When Copley's Youth, ſwift-ſtruggling thro' the wave,
The anxious boatmen ſtrain each nerve to ſave ;
As ſtrives the ravenous ſhark to reach his prey,
One lifts the javelin to arreſt his way ;
And now, as near his dreadful jaws expand,
One caſts the cord, and one extends the hand :
What care, what pity, mark their eager eyes !
What hopes, what terrors, in our boſoms riſe † !

---

　* Vide Weſt's celebrated Picture of the Death of General
Wolfe, engraved by Woollett.

　† See Mr. Copley's Picture of a Youth reſcued by Sailors
from a Shark in the Harbour of the Havannah. There is a fine
Mezzotinto of this Piece by Green.

　　　　　　　　　　　　　　The

The ſkilful Painter, at whoſe option lie

Poſitions various, fails not all to try;

And thoſe prefers, where every part the beſt

Accordance keeps, illuſtrating the reſt.

By different modes effect he oft obtains;

To one Chief Figure now the attention gains;

Now force on Second Characters beſtows,

And all his meaning by reflection ſhows;

Now thro' the Whole, each rank, and ſex, and age,

One common ruling paſſion bids engage.

When RAFFAELLE's SAVIOUR from the tomb

        aſcends,

Such majeſty and grace his preſence blends,

That the fix'd eye contemplates him alone,

Nor heeds the aſtoniſh'd guards around him thrown *.

When VANDYKE's General, whoſe victorious ſpear

Sunk Perſia's pride, and check'd the Goth's career,

---

* Raffaelle's Picture of the Refurrection of Chriſt; en-
graved by Vivarez and Grignion from a Drawing of Dalton.

Of fervice paid with indigence complains,

And fightlefs age on daily alms fuftains;

As the young Chief the affecting fcene furveys,

How all his form the emotion'd foul betrays!

' O thus has Fortune for the brave decreed?

' Of toils and dangers this at laft the meed * ?'

   When Rome's fair Princefs, who from Syria's fhore

Her late-loft Confort's facred afhes bore,

With fteps flow-moving o'er Brundufium's ftrand,

Meets her lov'd friends--a numerous mourning band--

Her gentle frame no geftures rude difgrace,

No vulgar grief deforms her beauteous face;

Her downcaft eyes immoveable remain,

Fix'd on the urn her careful hands fuftain.

The widow'd mother, by her garment's folds,

Clofe on each fide each tender offspring holds;

While Melancholy all the train o'erfhades

Of hoary warriors and of blooming maids;

---

* Vide the Belifarius of Vandyke; engraved by Goupy and
Scotin.

And

And all their breasts with pity seem to heave,

And for the dead and for the living grieve *.

The Great Sublime with energy to express

Exert thy utmost power, nor fear excess.

When Passion's tumults in the bosom rise,

Inflate the features, and enrage the eyes;

To Nature's outline can we draw too true,

Or Nature's colours give too full to view?

Did REYNOLDS' hand with force too strong disclose

Those looks that mark the unutterable woes,

When UGOLINE the wretch in prison lies,

And hears his dying children's piercing cries,

And while fell Hunger haunts the impervious

     walls,

And one by one the suffering victims calls,

---

* This capital Picture of Agrippina landing at Brundusium, with the ashes of Germanicus, is, in the Author's opinion, one of Mr. West's most pleasing compositions. There is a beautiful Print of it by Earlom.

Invokes

Invokes the lightning's bolt thofe walls to rend,

Or earth to open, and his miferies end * ?

Our Bards indeed, I own, here often fail,

And fpoil with bombaft and conceit their tale ;

Their heroes rant in many a curious ftrain

Of thought, that none could think in anger or in

pain.

Celeftial fcenes with caution muft be tried,

Where Knowledge fails, and Fancy fole can guide :

The Great Firft Caufe no form reveals to fight,

We mark his prefence by excefs of light † ;

While angel fhapes at eafe on wing remain,

Or on thin clouds their airy fteps fuftain.

---

* Vide Sir Jofhua Reynolds's excellent Picture of Count Ugolino and his Children in the Dungeon ; where they were confined and ftarved to death by the archbifhop Ruggieri. This circumftance is defcribed by the Italian poet Dantè.

† The Author could not here omit cenfuring the practice of fome celebrated Painters, who have prefumptuoufly and abfurdly reprefented the Supreme Being in the form of an Aged Man.

But

But tho', fair Painting! thus by juft defign,

And ftrong expreffion, much to pleafe is thine;

Yet not from thefe thy utmoft praifes rife,

For ufeful moral oft thy work fupplies.

When, 'midft Poussin's Arcadian vale ferene,

The virgin's fculptur'd monument is feen,

And the fad fhepherd pointing feems to fay,

' O Death, no place is facred from thy fway!'

Our mournful thoughts the well-known truth recal,

That Youth and Beauty oft untimely fall *.

On Carthage' plains when Marius meets the eye,

And the ftern Prætor's mandate bids him fly;

Frefh from the view the ftrong reflection fprings,

How ftrange the vaft viciffitude of things!

* Vide Pouffin's Picture, called The Shepherds in Arcadia; engraved by Ravenet, in Mr. Boydell's Collection of Prints: Alfo the Abbé Du Bos's Reflections on Poetry, Painting, and Mufic; and Dr. Warton's ingenious Effay on Didactic Poetry, in his Tranflation of Virgil.

X   Rome's

Rome's rival City to the duſt depreſt;

Her haughty Conſul there denied to reſt * !

When Perſia's Conqueror, 'midſt her female train,

Appears the chaſte, the generous, and humane;

His look, his action, on the mind impreſs

The needful knowledge how to bear ſucceſs †.

Thus may thy Art, O Friend, for ever prove

Of force, to Virtue, and from Vice, to move!

To Stateſmen, thoughtleſs on the heights of
          pow'r,

Mark Wolsey's fall, or ſhow his final hour;

To Patriot eyes give Marvell's calm diſdain,

When Danby urg'd the tempting bribe in vain ‡ ;

* There is a fine Picture of Mortimer's on this ſubject. The reply of Marius, to the meſſenger who came with orders for him to depart, was nobly concife and affecting: " Go, tell the Præ-
" tor, thou haſt ſeen Marius ſitting on the ruins of Carthage."

† Vide Le Brun's Alexander in the Tent of Darius, engraved by Edelinck.

‡ See the Life of Andrew Marvell, in Cibber's Lives of the Poets.

Or

Or bid the Inconftant her own doom deplore

In the fad exit of the haplefs SHORE *.

Without the Entheus Nature's felf beftows,

The world no Painter nor no Poet knows :

But think not Mind in its own depth contains

A fource of wealth that no difburfement drains :

Quick Obfervation, ever on the wing,

Home, like the bee, its ufeful ftores muft bring ;

From hills, and vales, and rocks, and ftreams, and

    trees,

And towns, and all that people thofe and thefe ;

From meaneft objects that may hints infpire,

Difcolour'd walls, or heaps of glowing fire †.

Care too befide thee ftill muft take her place,

Retouch each ftroke, and polifh every grace ;

* The interview between Shore and her Hufband, in the laft
fcene of Rowe's Tragedy, would afford a fine Picture.

† Vide Reynolds's Difcourfes, p. 61.

X 2

For when we join not dignity with eaſe,

Nor thou canſt paint, nor I can write, to pleaſe.

Perfection's point the Artiſt neareſt gains,

Who with his work unſatisfied remains:

Da Vinci's thought an excellence conceiv'd,

That his eye miſs'd in all his hand atchiev'd *.

The Clear-obſcure how happieſt to produce,

And what of various tints the various uſe,

My lay to that preſumes not to aſpire,

Nor with trite precept this thy ear ſhall tire:

Coreggio's practice that deſcribes the beſt;

In Freſnoy's theory this we find expreſt.

No rude incongruence ſhould thy piece diſgrace,

No motley modes of different time and place;

By Grecian chiefs no Gallic airs be worn †,

Nor in their hands be modern weapons borne;

* Vide Graham's Account of Painters, in Dryden's Freſnoy, p. 278.

† Vide Reynolds's Diſcourſes, p. 87.

Nor

Nor mix the crefted helm and coat of mail

With the vaft curl'd peruke, or pointed tail.

And facred ever be the folemn fcene

From bafe intrufion of burlefque and mean;

Nor in a Patriarch's or Apoftle's fight

Set fnarling dogs and growling cats to fight.

One caution further muft the Mufe impart;

Shun Naked Form, that fcandal of thy art:

Even DRYDEN blames them who refufe to fpare

The painful blufhes of the modeft Fair.

Let Decency her veil of drapery throw,

And Grace diffufe its folds in eafy flow *.

And now, my Friend, for Thee may Fortune

find

Employ congenial to thy liberal mind;

* Vide Dryden's Preface to his Tranflation of Frefnoy's Art
of Painting, p. 22, &c. where the licence of Painters, in the
above refpect, is feverely cenfured.

X 3   Not

Not taſks impos'd by power, or choſen for gain,

Begun reluctant, and purſued with pain.

What warms the heart, the hand with force reveals,

And all that force the charm'd ſpectator feels:

For Genius, piercing as the electric fiame,

When wak'd in one, in others wakes the ſame.

SONNETS

MISCELLANEOUS PIECES.

The following Sonnets, and the Stanzas addreſſed to Mrs. Macaulay, appeared in Pearch's Collection of Poems, publiſhed in 1770. The remaining Pieces are now firſt printed.

South View of Ware from ye Garden at Amwell.

SONNETS.

SONNET I.

APOLOGY FOR RETIREMENT. 1766.

WHY afks my Friend what cheers my paffing day,
　　Where thefe lone fields my rural home inclofe,
That all the pomp the crowded City fhows
Ne'er from that home allures my fteps away?

　Now thro' the upland fhade I mufing ftray,
And catch the gale that o'er the woodbine blows;
Now in the meads on river banks repofe,
And breathe rich odour from the new-mown hay:

　Now pleas'd I read the poet's lofty lay,
Where mufic fraught with ufeful knowledge flows;
Now DELIA's converfe makes the moments gay,
The Maid for love and innocence I chofe:
O Friend! the man who joys like thefe can tafte,
On vice and folly needs no hour to wafte.

S O N N E T II.

TO DELIA. 1766.

––––––––––

THRICE has the Year its varied circuit run,

   And fwiftly, DELIA, have the moments flown

Since with my love for Thee my care begun,

To improve thy tender mind to fcience prone.

  The flatteries of my fex I bade Thee fhun,

I bade Thee fhun the manners of thy own;

Fictitious manners, by example won,

That ill for lofs of innocence atone!

  Say, generous Maiden, in whofe gentle breaft

Dwells fimple Nature, undifguis'd by Art,

Now amply tried by Time's unerring teft,

How juft the dictates of this faithful heart;

Which, with the joys thy favouring fmiles impart,

Deems all its care repaid, itfelf fupremely bleft!

SONNET III.

AFTER READING SHENSTONE'S ELEGIES. 1766.

THE gentle SHENSTONE much of Fortune 'plain'd,
   Where Nature's hand the liberal ſpirit gave;
Partial, her bounty ſhe too oft reſtrain'd,
But pour'd it full on Folly's taſteleſs ſlave.

By her alike my humble prayer diſdàin'd,
She ſtern denies the only boon I crave;
O'er my fields, fair as thoſe Elyſian feign'd,
To bid the green walk wind, the green wood wave.

On the high hill to raiſe the higher tower,
To ope wide proſpects over diſtant plains,
Where by broad rivers towns and villas riſe;
Taſte prompts the wiſh, but Fortune bounds the power:
Yet while Health cheers, and Competence ſuſtains,
Theſe more than all, Contentment bids me prize.

S O N N E T IV.

PREFIXED TO LANGHORNE'S POETICAL WORKS. 1766.

───────────

Langhorne! unknown to me (fequefter'd fwain!)
 Save by the Mufe's foul-enchanting lay,
To kindred fpirits never fung in vain ;
Accept the tribute of this light effay.

 Sweet are thy fongs, they oft amufe my day ;
Of Fancy's vifions while I hear thee 'plain,
While Scotland's honours claim thy paftoral ftrain,
Or Mufic comes o'er HANDEL tears to pay.

 For all thy Irwan's flowery banks difplay,
Thy Perfian Lover, and his Indian fair ;
For all THEODOSIUS' mournful lines convey,
When Pride and Avarice part a matchlefs Pair ;
Receive juft praife, and wreaths that ne'er decay,
By Fame and Virtue twin'd for thee to wear.

S O N N E T V.

TO BRITAIN. 1766.

———————

RENOWN'D Britannia! lov'd Parental Land!
    Regard thy welfare with a watchful eye!
Whene'er the weight of Want's afflicting hand
Wakes in thy vales the Poor's perfuasive cry—

When wealth enormous fets the Oppreffor high,
When bribes thy ductile fenators command,
And flaves in office freemen's rights withftand;
Then mourn, for then thy fate approacheth nigh!

Not from perfidious Gaul or haughty Spain,
Nor all the neighbouring nations of the main,
Tho' leagued in war tremendous round thy fhore—
But from Thyfelf, thy ruin muft proceed!
Nor boaft thy power; for know it is decreed,
Thy freedom loft, thy power fhall be no more!

MISCELLANEOUS PIECES.

STANZAS

ON READING MRS. MACAULAY'S HISTORY OF
ENGLAND. 1766.

TO Albion's bards the Muſe of Hiſtory ſpoke:
     ' Record the glories of your native land,
' How Power's rude chain her ſons' brave efforts
       ' broke,
' And the keen ſcourge tore from Oppreſſion's hand.

     ' Give to renown the Patriot's noble deeds;
' Brand with diſgrace the Tyrant's hated name;
' Tho' Falſehood oft awhile the mind miſleads,
' Impartial Time beſtows impartial fame.'

She

She faid; and foon the lofty lyre they ftrung,

But artful chang'd the fubject and the lore;

Of kings, and courts, and courtly flaves they fung,

And glofs'd with vain applaufe their actions o'er.

The fervile ftrain the Mufe indignant heard;

Anxious for truth, for public virtue warm,

She Freedom's faithful advocate appear'd,

And bore on earth the fair MACAULAY's form.

E L E G Y

IN THE MANNER OF HAMMOND;

SUPPOSED TO HAVE BEEN WRITTEN IN THE AUTHOR'S
GARDEN, DURING A STORM. 1756.

BLOW on, ye Winds! exert your utmoſt rage,
 Sweep o'er the dome, or thro' the foreſt howl!
Could North with South, or Eaſt with Weſt engage,
 What were their war to that within my ſoul?

 There adverſe paſſions fierce contention hold,
 There Love and Pride maintain alternate ſway,
 There fell Deſpair's dark clouds on clouds are roll'd,
 And veil Hope's tranſient, faint, deluſive ray!

 Too charming SYLVIA! dear capricious Fair!
 What ſtrange perplexing change of mind is thine!
 No more thy ſmiles I'll truſt, thy frowns I'll bear;
 I'll ſhun the beauty that muſt ne'er be mine!

5

Was

Was it for thee I form'd this fair retreat,

Bade thro' the grove the smooth walk wind away,

Adorn'd that walk with many a rustic seat,

And by those seats bade tinkling runnels stray;

Along my sunny wall the fruit-tree spread,

Upon my eves expos'd the curling vine,

Around my door the spicy woodbine led,

Beneath my window saw the jasmine twine?

Blow on, ye Winds! exert your utmost power,

Rage thro' my groves, and bear down every tree;

Blast the fair fruit, and crush the blooming flower—

For Sylvia's lost, and these are nought to me!

Y

THE AUTHOR TO HIS WIFE. 1776.

FRIEND of my heart, by favouring Heaven be-
    stow'd,

My lov'd Companion on Life's various road!

Now fix fwift years have wing'd their flight away

Since yon bright Sun adorn'd our nuptial day——

For thy fweet fmiles, that all my cares remove,

Sooth all my griefs, and all my joys improve;

For thy fweet converfe, ever fram'd to pleafe,

With prudence lively, fenfible with eafe;

To Thee the Mufe awakes her tuneful lay,

The thanks of gratitude fincere to pay!

Thus long may HYMEN hold for us his reign,

And twine with wreaths of flowers his eafy chain;

Still may fond love and firmeft faith be mine,

Still health, and peace, and happinefs be thine!

4

STANZAS

WRITTEN AT MEDHURST IN SUSSEX, ON THE AU-
THOR'S RETURN FROM CHICHESTER, WHERE HE
HAD ATTEMPTED IN VAIN TO FIND THE BURIAL-
PLACE OF COLLINS.

TO view the beauties of my native land,
    O'er many a pleafing diftant fcene I rove;
Now climb the rock, or wander on the ftrand,
Or trace the rill, or penetrate the grove.

From Baia's hills, from Portfea's fpreading wave,
    To fair Ciceftria's lonely walls I ftray;
To her fam'd Poet's venerated grave,
    Anxious my tribute of refpect to pay *.

---

* Collins was born at Chichefter, died, and probably was
interred there.

O'er

O'er the dim pavement of the folemn fane,
'Midſt the rude ſtones that crowd the adjoining ſpace,
The ſacred ſpot I ſeek, but ſeek in vain;
In vain I aſk—for none can point the place.

What boots tne eye whoſe quick obſervant glance
Marks every nobler, every fairer form?
What the ſkill'd ear that ſound's ſweet charms in-
    trance,
And the fond breaſt with generous paſſion warm?

What boots the power each image to pourtray,
The power with force each feeling to expreſs?
How vain the hope that thro' Life's little day,
The ſoul with thought of future fame can bleſs?

While Folly frequent boaſts the inſculptur'd tomb,
By Flattery's pen inſcrib'd with purchas'd praiſe;
While Ruſtic Labour's undiſtinguiſh'd doom
Fond Friendſhip's hand records in humble phraſe;

5   Of

Of Genius oft and Learning worfe the lot;

For them no care, to them no honour fhown * :

Alive neglected, and when dead forgot,

Even COLLINS flumbers in a grave unknown.

Flow, Lavant, flow! along thy fedgy fhore

Bear the fraught veffel from the neighbouring main!

Enrich thy fons!—but on thy banks no more

May lofty Poet breathe his tuneful ftrain!

---

* This cenfure may feem too general—perhaps it is fo. But muft it not be allowed that the Public is capricious in beftowing its honours? Does not Weftminfter Abbey fhow monuments erected to men, as poets, who had little or no title to the name, while it contains no memorials of writers of far fuperior merit?

VERSES

TO A FRIEND, PLANTING.

PROCEED, my Friend, pursue thy healthful toil,

   Dispose thy ground, and meliorate thy soil;

Range thy young plants in walks, or clumps, or bowers,

Diffuse o'er sunny banks thy fragrant flowers;

And, while the new creation round thee springs,

Enjoy uncheck'd the guiltless bliss it brings:

But hope no more. Tho' Fancy forward stray

There scenes of distant pleasure to survey,

To expatiate fondly o'er the future grove,

The happy haunt of Friendship and of Love;

Know, each fair image form'd within thy mind,

Far wide of truth thy sickening sight shall find!

TO AN ABSENT FRIEND.

WHILE thou far hence on Albion's fouthern
       fhore,
View'ft her white rocks, and hear'ft her ocean roar;
Thro' fcenes, where we together ftray'd, I ftray,
And think o'er talk of many a long-paft day.

That favourite park now tempts my fteps again,
On whofe green turf fo oft at eafe we have lain;
While Hertford's turrets rofe in profpect fair,
And my fond thought beheld my SYLVIA there;
And much the Mufe rehears'd in carelefs lays
The Lover's fufferings and the Beauty's praife.

Thofe elm-crown'd fields now oft my walk invite,
Whence Lee's wide vale lies pleafant to the fight;
Where, as our view o'er towns and villas roll'd,
Our fancy imag'd how they look'd of old;

When

When Gothic manſions there uprear'd their towers,
Their halls for banquet, and for reſt their bowers.

But, O my Friend! whene'er I ſeek theſe ſcenes
Of lovely proſpects and delightful greens;
Regardleſs idly of the joy poſſeſs'd,
I dream of days to come, of days more bleſt,
When thou with me ſhalt wander here once more,
And we ſhall talk again our favourite topics o'er.

On Time's ſmooth current as we glide along,
Thus Expectation ever tunes her ſong:
' Fair theſe green banks with gaudy flow'rets bloom,
' Sweet breathe theſe gales, diffuſing rich perfume;
' Heed, heed them not, but careleſsly paſs by,
' To-morrow fairer, ſweeter will ſupply.'
To-morrow comes—the ſame the Syren's lay—
  To-morrow ſweeter gales, and flow'rets ſtill more gay.'

THE SHEPHERD's ELEGY;

OCCASIONED BY THE DEATH OF AN INGE-
NIOUS FRIEND.

UPON a bank with spreading boughs o'erhung,
    Of pollard oak, brown elm, and hornbeam grey,
The faded fern and russet grass among,
While rude winds swept the yellow leaves away,
And scatter'd o'er the ground the wild fruits lay;
As from the churchyard came the village throng,
Down sat a rural bard, and rais'd his mournful song.

' Nature's best gifts, alas, in vain we prize!
' The powers that please, the powers that pleasure gain!
' For O with them, in full proportion, rise
' The powers of giving and of feeling pain!
' Why from my breast now bursts this plaintive strain?
                                    ' Genius,

' Genius, my Friend! with all its charms was thine,
' And fenfibility too exquifite is mine!

  ' There low he lies!—that head in duft repos'd,
' Whofe active thought fcann'd every various theme!
' Clos'd is that eye, for ever, ever clos'd,
' Whence wont the blaze of fentiment to beam!
' Mute is that tongue, whence flow'd the copious
      ' ftream
' Of eloquence, whofe moral lore fo rare
' Delighted and improv'd the liftening Young and
      ' Fair.

  ' Witnefs for me, ye rain-polluted rills;
' Ye defart meads, that one brown hue difplay;
' Ye rude eaft-winds, whofe breath the dank air chills;
' Ye hovering clouds, that veil the Sun's faint ray!
' Witnefs, as annual here my fteps fhall ftray,
' How his dear image thought fhall ftill recall,
' And oft the figh fhall heave, and oft the tear fhall fall!'

A

As ceaſe the murmurs of the mantling pool,

As ceaſe the whiſpers of the poplar ſpray,

While o'er the vale the white miſt riſes cool

At the calm ſunſet of a ſummer's day—

So ſoftly, ſweetly ceas'd the Shepherd's lay :

While down the pathway to the hamlet plain

Return'd, with lingering ſteps, the penſive rural train.

ON THE

INGENIOUS MR. JONES'S ELEGANT TRANSLATIONS
AND IMITATIONS OF EASTERN POETRY, AND
HIS RESOLUTION TO DECLINE TRANSLATING THE
PERSIAN POETS.

THE Afian Mufe, a Stranger fair!

Becomes at length Britannia's care;

And HAFIZ' lays, and SADI's ftrains,

Refound along our Thames's plains.

They fing not all of ftreams and bowers,

Or banquet fcenes, or focial hours;

Nor all of Beauty's blooming charms,

Or War's rude fields, or feats of arms;

But Freedom's lofty notes fincere,

And Virtue's moral lore fevere.

But

But ah! they fing for us no more!

The fcarcely-tafted pleafure's o'er!

For He, the Bard whofe tuneful art

Can beft their varied themes impart—

For He, alas! the tafk declines;

And Tafte, at lofs irreparable, repines.

CONCLUSION.

TO A FRIEND.

———————————

WHEN erſt the Enthuſiaſt Fancy's reign
    Indulg'd the wild, romantic thought,
That wander'd 'midſt Arcadian vales,
Sicilian ſtreams, Arabian gales;
Bleſt climes, with wond'rous pleaſures fraught,
Sweet pleaſures, unalloy'd with pain!

    When Obſervation's calmer view
Remark'd the real ſtate of things;
Whate'er amuſive one obtain'd,
Whate'er of uſe the other gain'd,
To thee my verſe a tribute brings,
A tribute to thy friendſhip due.

                        Accept

Accept then this, nor more require :

The Mufe no further tafk effays ;

But 'midft the fylvan fcenes fhe loves,

The falling rills, and whifpering groves,

With fmiles her labours paft furveys,

And quits the fyrinx and the lyre *.

* See the Frontifpiece.

POSTSCRIPT.

THE Author, in the courfe of his literary enquiries, has had reafon to believe that the productions of fome writers have not unfrequently received very confiderable alterations and improvements from the hands of their friends. What he has been told of others, may poffibly be fufpected of himfelf; he therefore takes the liberty to obferve, that, although he has often derived advantage from the judicious remarks of a few kind acquaintance, to whom his MSS. have been fhown, he is not indebted to them, nor indeed to any perfon, for the infertion of a fingle line.

From the Works of preceding Poets, Memory has fometimes fupplied him with turns of expreffion, which, at the inflant of compofing, he imagined were his own; and at other times he has happened on lines ufed by Writers, whofe performances he had not then feen. Some inflances of fuch unconfcious plagiarifm, and accidental coincidence, are here pointed out, as matter of curiofity; others

Z   may

may poffibly exift, though he is not apprized of them.

> Blows not a flow'ret in the enamell'd vale,
> Shines not a pebble, &c.
>> *Elegies Defcriptive and Moral,* p. 27.

> Lurks not a ftone enrich'd with lively ftain,
> Blooms not a flower amid the vernal ftore,
> Falls not a plume on India's diftant plain,
> Glows not a fhell on Adria's rocky fhore—
>> SHENSTONE's *Works,* vol. i. 8vo. p. 140.

Perhaps SHENSTONE was indebted to AKENSIDE:

> ————Not a breeze
> Flies o'er the meadow, not a cloud imbibes
> The fetting Sun's effulgence, not a ftrain
> From all the tenants of the warbling fhade
> Afcends————
>> *Pleafures of Imagination,* book iii. line 593,

> But claims their wonder and excites their praife.
>> *Elegies Defcriptive and Moral,* p. 27.

> Provoke our wonder and tranfcend our praife.
>> ADDISON *to* DRYDEN, *Works,* vol. i. p. 3.

> Or rear the new-bound fheaves along the lands.
>> *Elegies Defcriptive and Moral,* p. 35.

> Or range my fheaves along the funny land.
>> HAMMOND, *Elegy* xiii. l. 12.

No more thofe noftrils breathe the vital air.
> *Elegies Defcriptive and Moral,* p. 44.

That while my noftrils draw the vital air.
> POPE, *Rape of the Lock,* canto iv.

In one fad fpot where kindred afhes lie.
> *Elegy written at Amwell,* 1763, p. 51.

In one lone fpot their mouldering afhes lie.
> *Mr.* KEATE's *Ruins of Netley Abbey,* 1764.

Of claffic lore accompanied my walk.   *Amwell,* p. 74

In fumptuous cars accompanied his march.
> LEONIDAS, book viii.

And his wild eye-balls roll with horrid glare.
> *Arabian Eclogue,* p. 133.

And his red eye-balls roll with living fire.
> DRYDEN's *Meleager and Atalanta.*

And one forlorn inhabitant contain'd.
> *Indian Eclogue,* p. 146.

The cities no inhabitant contain'd.
> FAWKES's *Song of Deborah;* *Poems,* p. 100.

Again he look'd, again he figh'd.   *Ode* ii. p. 173.

And figh'd and look'd— DRYDEN's *Alexander's Feaft.*

There Poverty, grim fpectre! rofe.   *Ode* xxi. p. 226.

Scar'd at the fpectre of pale Poverty.
> POPE, *Imitation of Horace,* book ii. epift. 1.

Each

Each paftoral fight, and every paftoral found.

Epiftle i. **p. 264.**

Defignedly imitated from MILTON:

Each rural fight, each rural found.——

And pure as vernal bloffoms newly blown.

Elegy written at Amwell, 1768.

All pure as bloffoms which are newly blown.

WM. BROWNE'*s Britannia's Paftorals,* vol. i. **p. 101.**

DAVIES's Edition of BROWNE's Works was pub-
lifhed in 1772. The Author had never feen any of
the old editions, nor any extract from them.

Hafte, bring my fteed fupreme in ftrength and grace,
Firft in the fight, and fleeteft in the chace.

Arabian Eclogue, **p. 133.**

This Eclogue was written in 1777. In a volume
of Poems by the ingenious Mr. MAURICE, printed
in 1779, the Author met with the following near
refemblance:

Full fifty fteeds I boaft of fwifteft pace,
Fierce in the fight, and foremoft in the race.

In the Amoebaean Eclogue, intitled THE DE-
SCRIBERS, p. 99, 100, a part of the imagery bears

a cona confiderable refemblance to fome defcriptions in a little collection of pleafing fonnets, by Mr. BAM-FYLDE, 1778; which collection the Author never faw till after his own volume was printed. This is a proof, that two writers, both painting from Na-ture, will often unknowingly coincide very nearly in feleétion, arrangement, and expreffion.

F I N I S.